For Paras

The Money Types
Guidebook

*Keep making
the magic happen!
Warmest wishes,*

Olivia Stefanino

Olivia xo

"Money is a medium for life - and when we begin to understand our emotional relationship with money, everything else in life suddenly starts to make sense too."

– *Olivia Stefanino*

CONTENTS

Foreword   7

Introduction   9

How to get the most out of this book...   11

Use this quiz to discover your 'Money Type'   14

Understanding your scores   16

Section 1: The 'Money Types'   **17**

    In brief   18

    The Pharaoh   20

    The Magician   41

    The Joker   63

    The Angel   84

    The Architect   105

    The Prisoner   126

Section 2: Coaching Stories   **147**

Section 3: The Money Stories   **172**

About the Author   204

WHAT OTHERS ARE SAYING

"Olivia has always had an intuitive gift for identifying and resolving the problems that have stopped individuals and teams from achieving their full potential. But it's the introduction of her remarkable 'Money Types' system that's going to take things to a whole new - world class - level.

Geoff Holt MBE DL, author of "Walking on Water"

"The Money Types' is really a book about emotions and consciousness because these deeper aspects of ourselves determine our financial behaviour. Olivia has drawn on her vast experience spanning both the personal development and financial sectors to create this insightful guide that is fun, well written and bound to give you a few 'aha' moments that you can put into action immediately."

Dr Manjir Samanta-Laughton MBBS, Dip-Bio-energy. author of "Punk Science" and "The Genius Groove".

"Olivia's insights are nothing short of breathtaking."

Noel Guilford, author of "How to Build a Successful Business"

"Relationships are the currency of life and finally here's a practical guidebook that inspires us to understand ourselves and others. It's comprehensive yet easy to understand - and equips leaders with the skills to see what's really going on under the surface."

Molly Harvey, author of "Outstanding Leadership"

"Olivia is deeply knowledgable and instinctive when it comes to understanding money and what it means in how we show up in the world. I was blown away by Olivia when she took me through my 'Money Types', so much so I booked her to be a speaker at my next International Women's Day Conference."

Sandra Green, author of "Handbags in the Boardroom" and founder of the Women Leaders Association

"Olivia has created a smart, accessible system that unpacks beliefs, values and behaviours, centred around our relationship with money and the impact it has on all of us. Insightful wisdom that elucidates the modern and complex world of Money Types."

Kala Flynn, author of "The Power of Human Energy"

"The 'Money Types' is the system I love using with clients because it really works. It helps reveal a whole other aspect to human behaviour.'"

Tianne Croshaw, contributing author of "Organisational Change Explained"

"Olivia is one of the most inspirational people you could ever get around."

Rob Brown - TEDx Speaker and author of "Build Your Reputation"

"Olivia provides the forum for the truth, sometimes a hard truth, to be revealed. It's never about the money and her 'Money Types' sessions reveal those hidden places that when brought to light, generate gold."

Jennifer Urezzio, author of "Soul Language"

FOREWORD

Money - so useful yet so misunderstood and misrepresented.

The vast majority of us weren't taught about money at school. Yes, we may have learned counting and maths - but that is only a fragment of what money is *really* about. Consequently, most people don't speak the language of money.

At one level, we all know that money helps us to function in the practical day to day of life. At another much deeper level, mastering money is the art - or alchemy - of mastering ourselves. Used wisely, money acts like a mirror for who we really are. It can magnify certain personality traits, helping us to understand and transform ourselves. This book is about that emotional awareness and understanding.

Like the archetypes proposed by Carl Jung, Olivia's 'Money Types' reveal hidden forms within each of us. They show us the inner stories we tell ourselves not only about money - but more importantly about ourselves. They also shine a light in the darkness, revealing to us what we've hidden in our shadow.

As you work through this book, the improved relationship you'll begin to have with yourself will also enable you to see other people through fresh eyes. You'll have a greater understanding of who they are, what makes them tick and how similar they are to you. Similar hopes, similar fears, similar dreams. 'Divided by our differences or united by our similarities' now becomes a **conscious choice** - rather than us unconsciously playing out our previously uninvestigated stories and projecting them onto the people around us.

Jumping back in time slightly, when Olivia first 'birthed' the 'Money Types' system in 2013 for a seminar I was running, I admit we didn't initially recognise its power - or potential. It was only the excited reaction of the audience members who were eagerly pointing out just how many people could benefit from it - whether they were looking for business growth as leaders and managers or for personal growth as partners and parents -

that persuaded Olivia to develop it further. With more than twenty years' experience to draw on - both from her private practice and the extensive leadership and executive coaching work she's done with businesses - she's gone on to develop a remarkable body of work.

I now use the 'Money Types' with every client in my own Lifestyle Financial Planning business. It helps **me** to understand them quickly - and it helps **them** to understand themselves and each other in a new way. Couples who'd repeatedly been clashing - often over more than just money - were suddenly able to understand **why**. It was their different dominant 'Money Types' that had been causing the problems - and once they recognised this, they were able to find new, better ways of communicating with each other.

With her uncanny ability to tap into and provide deep insight into the human condition, Olivia understands why we wear the masks we do - and shows us how to drop them to reveal the authentic human being underneath.

In short, engaging with and applying the unique wisdom of the 'Money Types' promises to give us all a better life both at home and at work. As well as paying dividends for us as individuals and those closest to us, I believe it can also give us hope for humanity.

Simon Yates, *CFP Chartered MCSI DipPFS*

INTRODUCTION

"Each day, do all you can to create five wins: The first for yourself, the second for your loved ones, the third for your associates, the fourth for your community and the fifth for humanity."

Olivia Stefanino

You know, I just love it when I hear from clients, whether they're the ones who've finally discovered what was holding them back in business, the ones who've worked out how to get their teams running smoothly so that profits go up - or the ones who've finally had a breakthrough in their marriage.

And while I was getting this kind of positive feedback before the 'Money Types', it's only since their birth that I've started hearing the word 'enlightening' on numerous occasions.

Of course, my ego enjoys the positive strokes - I'll happily admit to still being a work-in-progress! And in truth, I can't take all the credit for the 'Money Types' themselves - after all they came 'through' me rather than 'from' me. I do however, feel extraordinarily honoured to be their Ambassador.

Wonderfully, the mission of the 'Money Types' team - the Pharaoh, Magician, Joker, Angel, Architect and Prisoner is now being fulfilled - as growing numbers of people are not only coming to understand **why** they behave the way they do but they're also quickly learning **how** to overcome their previously sabotaging behaviours.

Of course, we're able to understand others better when we first understand ourselves - and it's our relationships in life that create either happiness and success or misery and frustration. The lifeblood of relationships is communication - and the 'Money Types' system provides a fun 'common language' that's not only easy to learn, but helpfully, it's easy to remember too.

We all have a relationship with Money. Love it or loath it, it's woven into the infrastructure of our lives.

Earlier in my own life, the relationship I had with Money was truly awful. And while it may have taken me a while to get things back on an even keel, I'm now deeply grateful for the whole learning experience. Indeed, I've subsequently come to understand that **Money is arguably one of our greatest teachers** - that's all along been hidden in plain sight. When we begin to understand our emotional relationship with Money, everything else in life suddenly starts to make sense too. Money is a fabulous medium for understanding both ourselves and others - as it teaches us about our deeply hidden beliefs, drives and attitudes.

Of course, there are a number of very helpful profiling systems already out there. But the 'Money Types' is a different animal altogether. Each one of us has our own powerful **personal combination** of the Pharaoh, Magician, Joker, Angel, Architect and Prisoner and they all have their own role to play. As well as learning more about our particular gifts and talents and how to apply them positively in our lives, the 'shadow' side of the six 'Money Types' also has much to teach us about how to avoid the traps and pitfalls we so often find ourselves up against time and time again. Indeed, it's been this exploration into the 'shadow' that also helped me identify the nine most troublesome 'Money Stories' which, until we learn to transcend them, keep us trapped in a repeating cycle of negativity. I will of course be sharing more about all that I've discovered - but for now, I'll let you into a secret: it often has little to do with how much we've squirrelled away in savings or investments.

I really hope you enjoy and learn a lot from the rich information in this book - and let me leave you with one final thought. While many say that 'knowledge is power', my belief is that it's only when we choose to **apply** knowledge that the magic really happens.

Yours excitedly,

Olivia x

HOW TO GET THE MOST OUT OF THIS BOOK...

I suggest you do the quiz and apply the wisdom of the 'Money Types' to yourself first because frankly, it's easier to understand something when you're able to consider it through the lens of your own situation - rather than trying to learn it as an abstract concept.

So, before you do ANYTHING else, let me repeat: Complete the quiz on page 14 *first*! This will ensure that you're able to respond to the 'statements' with no bias.

(The good news is that each of the 'Money Types' has wisdom and gifts to share. By completing the quiz authentically from the outset, you're guaranteed to get the most out of everything the system has to offer.)

When you've completed the quiz, you'll then be armed with your personal 'Money Types' combination score. I've created a chapter for each of the six 'Money Types' in section 1 - and if you're like most people, you'll be wanting to learn everything about your primary 'Money Type' as soon as you can, so it makes sense to start with that chapter first.

Next, read through the other five chapters in Section 1, using the ranking of your 'Money Types' combination score to guide you.

You'll find the first couple of chapters you read - which correspond with your highest scores - will really feel uncannily 'like you'. The remaining chapters will of course, feel less and less 'like you' (which makes sense as they'll reflect your reducing 'Money Types' scores).

However, even if you have a low score for a specific 'Money Type', it's still really important that you read through the relevant chapter to ensure that you have a working knowledge of them *all*. As well as highlighting some of the qualities that you could perhaps benefit from developing within yourself, you'll find it immeasurably helpful to have a working knowledge of each 'Money Type' when it comes to understanding how other people tick. And wouldn't *that* be helpful?!

In Section 2, you'll get the chance to be a fly-on-the-wall when I share some coaching stories from my own private practice. Personally, I learn a lot from other people's stories - and I very much hope you will too.

Finally, in Section 3, I'll be sharing the nine 'Money Stories' that most often trip people up in life - along with some helpful 'Money Types' guidance.

And by way of conclusion for the book, you'll find Money's own wise words for each of the six 'Money Types'.

And just in case these questions are popping up for you too...

Finally, I'm always asked at least one of the following questions when I do a talk about the 'Money Types', so on the basis that some of them may be occurring to you too, let me share them (along with my responses) below:

1 **Are any of the six 'Money Types' better or preferable to any of the others?**

No! They all have equal value and much wisdom to share. It's also worth pointing out though, that they each have a 'light' and a 'shadow' side. Each has powerful gifts to bestow BUT each also can cause problems for the unwary!

2 **What happens if I have two 'highest' scores that are the same?**

Don't worry, it's quite common for people to have two (and very occasionally more!) primary 'Money Types'. When you read the relevant chapters, you'll find that both feel 'like you'. It's also worth considering whether you have your primary 'Money Types' working in harmony with each other, or whether you have one operating in its 'light' side, while the other is inadvertently operating from the 'shadow'. Understanding how this can play out is often very helpful - not least because it provides clues as to where and how you might be sabotaging yourself in life (and not just with money!).

3 Will my scores change over time?

Many people find that while their individual scores may change slightly, the overall 'order of ranking' of their 'Money Types' remains the same. However, a number of people have also found that as they continue on their own self-development journey, their scores go up for **all** the 'Money Types' - often because (even though they're unaware of it) they're starting to 'own' some of the attributes they had previously been ignoring.

4 How is this different from all the other profiling systems out there?

While there are many useful profiling tools out there, I've yet to come across one that uses **money** as the medium for understanding (and of course, it's not really about the money!).

Also, many tools compare your scores with those of thousands of others to compute your result - and reveal that you are either 'this' or 'that'. But with this system, it's *your* unique 'Money Types' ***combination*** (and knowing how to play to its strengths or avoid the traps) that's all-important. (Indeed, some people like to think of their six 'Money Types' as an 'internal Board of Directors' - in much the same way that Napoleon Hill first suggested in his famous book, *"Think and Grow Rich"*.)

But while your personal 'Money Types' combination is all that *you* need, I sense that you'll also find it encouraging to know that the 'Money Types' concept has been tested and proven over a number of years with a wide variety of organisations, teams, couples and individuals.

5 Can I ask my partner/family/friends to take the quiz too?

Absolutely! And if you don't want them writing in *your* book, you can invite them to join my FREE online community - The Vault Cafe - where they will be able to do the quiz for themselves (completely free). I'd love to welcome *you* to join our growing community too - to do so, simply follow this link: https://oliviastefanino.com/membership-registration

USE THIS QUIZ TO DISCOVER YOUR 'MONEY TYPE'

For each statement below with which you agree, score a '3'. Score a '0' for each statement with which you disagree - and for any statements with which you neither agree nor disagree (or which you don't feel fully apply to you) score a '1'. The 30 statements are broken down into 6 sections – add up your score for each section and write it in the appropriate section box on the right.

	AGREE 3	NEITHER 1	DISAGREE 0
SECTION 1:			
1. Being financially wealthy is the best form of security			
2. I want to be wealthier than the previous generation in my family			
3. I measure my happiness through my material success			
4. I want future generations to appreciate my success			
5. People admire me because of what I'm worth in material terms			
Section 1 Total:		9	
SECTION 2:			
1. I know I can rely on myself to create what I need and want in life			
2. I believe it's important to continue my education throughout my whole life			
3. Investing in myself and my personal development is a good use of money			
4. I can often spot opportunities that others miss			
5. People often describe me as 'entrepreneurial'			
Section 2 Total:		13	
SECTION 3:			
1. You never know what's around the corner, it's important to live for 'today'			
2. There's never enough money at the end of the month			
3. Socialising with my friends and family is extremely important to me			
4. I'm comfortable shopping for non-essential items on my credit card			
5. People love spending time in my company because we always have a good time			
Section 3 Total:		6	

	AGREE 3	NEITHER 1	DISAGREE 0

SECTION 4:

1. Looking after my family and friends is my priority
2. I enjoy organising and catering for special events
3. I'd rather spend my money on other people, as I like making them happy
4. Sometimes I find myself wondering when it's going to 'my turn' to get what I want
5. People say that I have great empathic skills and am very caring

Section 4 Total:		6	

SECTION 5:

1. I believe that success is the outcome of having clear goals
2. I like having a detailed plan for achieving what I want
3. Ever since I was young, I've been a 'saver'
4. While I appreciate beauty, I believe that 'function' is even more important than "form"
5. People describe me as a '"Steady Eddy' rather than as a 'Flash Harry'

Section 5 Total:		11	

SECTION 6:

1. Whatever I do, I never seem to make any progress financially
2. I am worried about what will happen when I get old
3. Whenever money comes my way, I often find a big bill comes in soon after
4. I see other people succeed and feel a little jealous that I don't share their luck
5. People often admit to feeling sorry for me

Section 6 Total:		2	

Now turn overleaf to work out your 'Money Types' combination...

UNDERSTANDING YOUR SCORES

Now look at your scores for each of the six sections – the section with the highest score reveals your primary 'Money Type', the next highest, your secondary 'Money Type' and so on. If you have two or more scores that are the same (irrespective of where they are in the 'pecking order') then these 'Money Types' are playing out equally in your life.

	YOUR SCORE (from previous two pages)	WHICH 'MONEY TYPE' APPLIES TO EACH SECTION	RANK EACH 'MONEY TYPE' (according to your scores... 1st, 2nd, 3rd etc)
Section 1:	4	PHAROAH	3
Section 2:	13	MAGICIAN	1
Section 3:	6	JOKER	4
Section 4:	6	ANGEL	4
Section 5:	11	ARCHITECT	2
Section 6:	0	PRISONER	0

If you prefer to do this key step digitally, you can easily do so by joining my FREE 'Vault Cafe' online community at: https://oliviastefanino.com/membership-registration

16

SECTION 1

Understanding each of the six
'Money Types' in more depth...

The *Pharaoh*

The *Magician*

The *Joker*

The *Angel*

The *Architect*

The *Prisoner*

IN BRIEF

The Pharaoh

AS A NATURAL LEADER, the Pharaoh has an aptitude for building wealth, governing their dominion with determination and prowess. With a clear personal vision for how things should be, the Pharaoh's successes attract others to their 'service'. Strong, focused, driven and articulate, successful Pharaohs 'rule' fairly - but they need to ensure that all their projects and endeavours result in a 'win-win' for everyone.

The Magician

AS A NATURAL ENTREPRENEUR, the Magician delights in spotting opportunities and creating out-of-the-box solutions for problems. Creativity drives the Magician - and figuring out how to build multiple income streams is a no-brainer! Intelligent, persuasive, optimistic and charismatic, successful Magicians are skilled at inspiring others with the vision - but they need to ensure that they focus and communicate clearly.

The Joker

AS A NATURAL CONNECTOR, the Joker loves connecting ideas with people - and people with people. Armed with their little black book, the Joker gets things done by knowing who can help! The Joker builds audiences - recognising that the 'goldmine' lies in the database. Fun, engaging, inspiring and popular, successful Jokers create an atmosphere of sunshine - but they need to remember to sustain momentum to keep everyone happy.

IN BRIEF

The Angel

AS A NATURAL COLLABORATOR, the Angel is dedicated to helping everyone around them - whether they're colleagues, clients or customers. Great listeners, counsellors and advisors, Angels attract fans who love to recommend and refer their products or services. Empathic, intuitive, warm and understanding, successful Angels focus on what others need and want - but they truly need to learn to look after themselves too.

The Architect

AS A NATURAL ORGANISER, the Architect excels at managing projects and people, using frameworks and checklists to measure progress. Often armed with a specialist skill or vocation, Architects love delving into the detail and they seek continuous personal improvement. Logical, practical, calm and efficient, successful Architects are able to anticipate problems before they occur - but they need to guard against demotivating others around them.

The Prisoner

AS A NATURAL FREEDOM-FIGHTER, the Prisoner focuses on what isn't working - which can bring about evolution (or revolution!). Feeling stuck and unhappy with the status quo, the successful Prisoner can both articulate what's wrong and determine the solution. Demanding, complaining, envious and exhausting, the Prisoner has the power to bring change - but needs to avoid moaning, step into their power and then take action.

THE PHARAOH

PHARAOHS have an innate aptitude for building wealth and are recognised as natural leaders. With their ability to repeatedly make big things happen, Pharaohs usually find themselves surrounded by plenty of people who are happy to help them build their vision.

What can help the PHARAOH: Focusing on creating 'win:win' opportunities for everyone in their community ensures that others see how helping the Pharaoh will help them too. Pharaohs first need to seek to understand what other people aspire to achieve for themselves – and then they should use this knowledge to inspire and encourage those around them to reach their goals (which, of course, they've taken care to align with their own.)

The trap that could undermine the PHARAOH: Building wealth is good, however in ancient Egypt, the Pharaohs concentrated on building wealth so that they could take it into the 'next world'. The trap is that by focusing primarily on 'money', Pharaohs fail to live the life they want in 'this world' - and while they may die rich, will they be happy with the lives they lived?

Three 'Insight Questions' for Pharaohs:

1. What will you regret not having done or experienced in your life because you were too focused on making money?

2. Are you building wealth because you're afraid that the money is going to run out?

3. Do you know the goals of the people who can help you achieve your vision and how together, you can create "win:win" situations?

PHARAOH GLOBAL ROLE: LEADER

Pharaohs are self-confident individuals who know - and who've always known - that their role is to take charge. Preferring to rely on themselves when it comes to taking decisions, wise Pharaohs know that they do well to surround themselves with clever and able people whose learning and expertise they can call upon.

From a young age Pharaohs challenge themselves to be the best - whatever their endeavour. Pharaohs are as at home on the sports field as they are in the executive office suite and whether or not they have the official title of 'boss', everybody knows who's at the top of the food chain.

Flamboyant and full of life, Pharaohs certainly aren't afraid to take their space in the world. On the contrary, they stride about confidently - going about their business with all the assurance of knowing that their word goes.

Unfortunately however, Pharaohs can fall into the trap of believing their own press releases - and they don't always know what they don't know. This can lead to costly mistakes, which of course the optimistically-minded Pharaoh simply refers to as 'learning opportunities'.

Their self-belief is so powerful that unintentionally, people can give away their own power to the Pharaoh, in the assumption that the latter must be right - after all, that's the vibe they give off. But the Pharaoh isn't always right - and on occasion, they can find themselves tripped up by their own hubris. (And when this occurs, they can blame the people around them for not forewarning them, although the probability is that the Pharaoh wouldn't have listened anyway.)

Whenever the Pharaoh is in town, they love people to know it. More than likely they'll turn up in a flashy car - but even if it's less showy than it could be, it'll still be reassuringly expensive.

Similarly, they dress to stand out - and they talk (often quite loudly) in a way that commands attention. Pharaohs expect to get what they want - and they don't expect other people's rules to get in the way. In a restaurant, if the menu doesn't suit them, they'll ask politely (but with a slight 'tone' that assumes they'll get their way) to go 'off-piste'. Equally, on aircraft or in hotels, they'll again have no compunction in asking for an upgrade - and more often than not, whenever it's possible, their wishes will be accommodated. For this reason, while they don't actually pay for it, Pharaohs often enjoy a better quality of life than everyone else - simply because they're not afraid to **ask**.

In order to thrive, Pharaohs need to win the hearts and minds of everyone in their tribe - ensuring that everyone's goals are neatly aligned.

Commonly referred to as 'Alpha' male or female, Pharaohs often have such belief in the importance of their projects that they can completely fail to take other people's **feelings** into account.

Over time, this can lead to resentment in the very people that Pharaohs believe they were put on the earth to lead. Pharaohs, who aren't always given to unbiased self-reflection, often find themselves bewildered when they encounter passive aggressiveness from within their entourage.

Indeed, it could even be said that Pharaohs often see the people around them as the 'instruments' for getting things accomplished. Not for nothing has it been said that all great civilisations were built on the 'backs of slaves'.

Perhaps surprisingly, the Pharaoh rather enjoys it when people stand up to them and debate their actions and decisions - and they respect the people who do. Well, unless they're having a 'bad day', in which case the Pharaoh can swiftly adopt an 'off with their head' mentality.

For this reason, Pharaohs can suffer from people being a bit wary of them - after all, which type of leader will they be dealing with today - the magnificent commander or the petty tyrant?

KEY ROLES: Leader, Politician, Orator

KEY BELIEF: "When I'm in charge, everyone is better off"

KEY LESSON: Making sure that 'win:win' situations are created

KEY STRENGTH: Self Belief

KEY DESIRE: Sovereignty

PHARAOH PERSONAL DRIVE: RULING

Pharaohs know that they were 'born to lead' - and sense this power from a young age. It never occurs to them that not everyone feels the same way or has the same experience in life and so, completely unintentionally, the Pharaoh can end up dominating people and situations. Some people around them are happy for them to take the lead, while others end up resentful.

While Pharaohs see it as their responsibility - and duty - to take care of those around them, they do expect people to step up to the plate themselves.

When Pharaohs understand that leadership is about serving rather than being served, their lives transform and become easy, successful and abundant...

As leaders, Pharaohs expect to guard their emotions - recognising that they need to be seen as 'strong' to retain their ruling status. They can't abide weakness or over-emotionality in others.

They can fall into the trap of leaning too much on their 'masculine side' (irrespective of whether they're male or female) in a bid to promote the 'strength' of their persona. For example, they find displays of (masculine) anger much more acceptable than (feminine) tearfulness - which they believe to be a vulnerability or weakness that should be hidden at all times.

This approach can lead other people to see the Pharaoh as cold or heartless, which often isn't true. It's just that they're afraid of the mask slipping - mistakenly, they perceive that it's the mask that holds the power.

Truly enlightened Pharaohs - and sadly there aren't so many of them - don't just allow the mask to slip, they make the choice to remove the mask altogether. They do this by going on an inner journey - doing the necessary self-development work and balancing their masculine and feminine powers.

And from this place of true strength, they step into their real sovereignty. No longer dependent on the mask, the Pharaoh is able to connect with the hearts and minds of everyone around them - and lead them to a land of fulfilment and success.

Finally, Pharaohs have a genuine and deep-seated belief that they **know** how the world should be. They often feel that they're being 'called' - and are responsible for - leading their vision of 'how life could and should be', which they carry as a blueprint deep within their being.

PHARAOH: RELATIONSHIP WITH MONEY

When it comes to making money, Pharaohs are the experts. They know that it 'takes money to make money' and one of their joys in life is building their portfolio.

Some Pharaohs get a head start in life - through a Trust fund, an inheritance or a slice of the family firm - but irrespective of what hand of cards they're dealt, they pride themselves on taking what they've got and making it grow.

Of course, Pharaohs don't spend all their time counting everything in their coffers, but they do have a sense of 'what they're worth' running through their minds on a continuous loop - and it's this constant reminder of their progress that gives them such confidence in life. While they're not averse to hard work themselves, Pharaohs recognise that nothing great can be achieved without a team. And of course, they expect to lead and direct that team themselves. Rather than swapping their own time for money - which is effectively what people who are employed do, Pharaohs know that there are three better ways to make BIG advances in their personal fortunes: Employ other people to work for them (and make a profit on their employees time); invest in property (there's a potential for both capital growth and rental income); invest in stocks and shares (again, there's potential for capital growth - together with dividend income. And of course, when dividend income is reinvested, one can achieve exponential growth. Pharaohs particularly like exponential growth.)

Pharaohs enjoy being able to display their wealth - and they often live in prestigious houses with the 'right address'. They know that first impressions count - for a lot - and leave everyone in no doubt as to their financial prowess.

Interior design is also important for the Pharaoh, for it gives them an opportunity to display their wealth in tasteful but often rather 'obvious' ways. Those who aren't sure of their own 'taste' when it comes to decor are perfectly happy to invest in the services of an interior designer.

Besides their 'castles', Pharaohs often have top model cars, which are always clean and polished. (They have a valet on speed-dial). On occasion they may even hire a chauffeur - often so they can sit in the back seat and make important phone calls or catch up on some reading or on occasion, just to make an impression.

Pharaohs expect to be wealthy - and perhaps it's for this reason that they so often are. After all, our external world is a reflection of our inner thoughts and beliefs.

Irrespective of whether they're male or female, with their innate sense of responsibility, Pharaohs expect to be the 'provider' when it comes to relationships. This is partly because it just feels natural - but they also have a strong belief that whoever holds the purse strings, holds the control. Control is very important to Pharaohs.

While they can be very generous - Pharaohs can throw lavish parties for example - they do struggle to share. They have no trouble 'giving' because that comes with a sense of power and largesse - 'sharing' however suggests equality, which is much tougher for a Pharaoh to handle. After all, with equality comes shared power and while they're not against that in principle, they just don't know how to handle not being able to call all the shots themselves. With practice (and a great deal of patience from everyone else) they can get there in the end, especially in a true love match.

Pharaohs teach that taking care of ourselves - looking after our own needs, wants and desires so that we don't burden others - is actually the most selfless gift we can share with the world.

While ultimately they'll end up running their own show, Pharaohs often learn their craft while working for other people in their younger years. Nevertheless, even from the outset, Pharaohs have a very clear understanding of their own value - which means that they can often end up earning more than their peers.

Why?

They know that when it comes to negotiating their own pay package, they need to strike a hard bargain at the beginning - and they do so by demonstrating how much profit they'll make for an organisation. They'll also have taken the trouble to find out what others - who work for an organisation's competitors - are paid and they know not to settle for a penny less.

Pharaohs know their worth and **demand** to be paid it!

Ideal careers for Pharaohs

Justice | Economics | Medicine | Media | Hospitality | Chef
Politics | Public Speaking | Entertainment

Pharaohs have a great sense of 'dynasty' - and they love nothing more than planning and creating wealth for the generations to come. They rather like the idea that even when they're long dead and buried, they'll be fondly remembered as the family's benefactor.

With the sheer amount of wealth that they build - often through complicated portfolios, trusts and even offshore accounts, Pharaohs often require a team of financial experts to help them 'run the money'. They see this as money well spent - and while others sometimes find discussions about money 'boring', Pharaohs absolutely love it.

Pharaohs often have no difficulty **displaying** their wealth - and almost see it as their duty - but not all of them find it as easy to **enjoy** the trappings of their success. Knowing how much they're 'worth' in pure numerical terms is a key driver for them - and they can equate **spending** money with the ignominy of seeing their personal 'value' reducing (at least on paper). This can lead to a few Pharaohs leading an austere life, while having millions in the bank. For these individuals, it's a case of recognising that life is to be lived **now**.

Pharaohs already have it pretty well sussed when it comes to making money - indeed, even as young adults most of them are already on their way to creating some serious wealth.

With their leadership abilities, they have no problem climbing the 'greasy pole' to success in corporate land if that's their preference. Knowing their worth, and being gifted with plenty of self confidence, means that they have no problem when it comes to negotiating a good deal for themselves.

Pharaohs often very much agree with what my beloved grandfather once told me, which is that while there's a limit to how much you can earn... there's no limit to how much you can make!

Also, Pharaohs definitely get what Albert Einstein meant when he said that, "Compound interest is the most powerful force in the Universe".

Pharaohs enjoy measuring their success...

Given that Pharaohs often enjoy measuring their success through how much they're worth, they're likely to get in on the investment game sooner rather than later - whether it's through the stock market, property or other people working for them. On occasion, they even manage to find a way of making all three elements happen simultaneously.

While we can achieve so much on our own, when we collaborate with others, BIG things happen.

Given that they're naturally leaders, Pharaohs particularly thrive when they're in a business partnership with a Magician. Pharaohs bring the gravitas, inspire the clients and rally the troops. They're also a massive asset when the organisation is looking to attract financial backers. Meanwhile, the entrepreneurial Magician has an uncanny ability to spot opportunities and to create the solutions to the problems prospective customers and clients didn't always even know they had.

To make this kind of business partnership work though, there needs to be mutual respect and a clear division of who is in charge of what. Too much cross-over will lead to arguments sooner rather than later. Finally, when it comes to looking after a Pharaoh's assets - they do well to bring in someone to do it for them. Yes, they could do it themselves but that's not really their style. And wonderfully, Pharaohs are wise enough to recognise the value of paying for specialist expertise when it comes to the things that really matter.

How to have difficult money conversations at home

Pharaohs like to feel in control and can be threatened by what they perceive as criticism if anyone but them instigates the conversation. Ask a Pharaoh to share their ideas on how they believe things should progress - and to take charge of ensuring that the conversations happen (which is very different to asking them to take charge of the conversation) - on a regular basis, and they're much more likely to play ball. Respectfully help them see that by working together, you can build a solid future, of which you can both be proud.

When it comes to talking about money in business

Pharaohs are completely comfortable talking about money in business - indeed, they often like to be seen to **pay the most** for the best service, because they know they deserve it.

However, someone in their Shadow Pharaoh often only sees things from their own perspective, which leads to them being overbearing and over-demanding.

The shadow can also play out when Pharaohs choose to measure their success with money - comparing themselves to others and wanting to 'trump' them by having more, or 'keeping more'. This doesn't always bode well for negotiations.

The Pharaoh's attitude to financial risk

Given that the Pharaoh measures his or her success in terms of wealth and the things they own, they are generally good at building up their coffers. While this means that they are likely to have a robust capacity for loss when it comes to maintaining their lifestyles - with their portfolios able to withstand a fall in the share market - emotionally, it's likely to be a somewhat different matter.

Having to admit to others - and particularly recognise for themselves - that they are now worth 'less on paper' than they were, is likely to cause upset.

Pharaohs (along with Prisoners) are the most likely to look for someone else to blame when things don't go as expected.

How to persuade or sell to the Pharaoh

The Pharaoh wants to feel special - and nothing makes them happier than feeling that they're worthy of being given VIP status.

It's also worth noting that they're very happy to pay handsomely for privileged service - after all, they want to be acknowledged as being in an 'elite'.

Having said that, if they feel that they're somehow in competition with the person selling to them, the Pharaoh's competitive side can come out and they'll fight hard to create a 'I win, you lose' scenario. (The fact that they're likely to lose out themselves in the long term - through the resentment they've created, never seems to occur to them.)

They like to be heard - and to feel confident that everyone is aware that the Pharaoh's opinion matters.

When producing printed literature, make sure that it's glossy, weighty and feels expensive if it's to appeal to the Pharaoh.

PHARAOH AT WORK: As the boss

Pharaoh bosses always lead from the front - and from the outset, there's no debate about who's in charge or who has the last word. Such is their self-belief, Pharaohs adopt the view that their way is the right way - and while for some of their tribe this provides a sense of trust and security, for others it can be extraordinarily frustrating.

Unused to being questioned, Pharaohs tend to expect their orders to be carried out with no fuss or complaint and they have little patience for people on the team who whinge and moan at every turn.

Pharaohs often have great speaking talents - and as the leader of their organisations, they can inspire their teams, their market place and their financial backers. People like to be associated with Pharaohs, often in the hope that a little bit of their wealth and magic will rub off on them.

They're also good at courting publicity - and recognise that public opinion can easily be swayed by the media. Pharaohs understand the importance of fashions and trends and ensure that they - and their organisations - are the ones being 'talked about'. They enjoy the attention - and they also know that where the 'media leads', the pennies will follow.

Pharaohs' personal style is to pace about their dominion - often flanked with their close entourage - making sure that everything is going according to plan. They have an uncanny eye for picking up on a tiny detail that's flawed - and enjoy making people run around to fix it. While this keeps standards up, it can lead to a demoralised team - as rarely are they congratulated for all their hard work, but are instead pulled up and castigated for something inconsequential.

Pharaohs believe that this behaviour keeps people on their toes, but actually what happens over time is that people try less and less hard, and end up doing as little as possible. This absolutely isn't because they're lazy - but because their spirit has been crushed. After all, if you know that your best efforts will still be criticised, why bother?

To counter this, Pharaohs need to understand just how important good morale is - and what they can do personally to boost it. Remembering people's names is a good start - and choosing to give credit where it's due can go a long way. Pharaohs also need to understand the wisdom of praising in public - but reprimanding in private. Sadly, they often get this the wrong way round.

Enlightened Pharaohs - those who have done some inner personal 'work' and who recognise that they're here to serve the world, rather than the world existing to serve them - are truly capable of leading the world to a brighter future.

As managers & colleagues

Pharaohs can be good at leading a team - providing they have a sense of 'ownership' about the end objective. They excel at working out what needs to be done and allocating tasks according to whoever's best for the job. Often, they leave themselves with less of the hard graft to do themselves and occupy themselves with 'overseeing'. This can be frustrating for those in their teams, who may feel more inspired by a 'leading from within' approach, in which everyone mucks in together.

However, it has to be said that the Pharaoh sometimes gets a bad rap in this regard. What the others on the team don't always see is how much the Pharaoh 'protects them' from the outside world, whether that's demanding bosses or irritated customers.

Pharaohs are also the ones who create relationships in high places - recognising that sometimes, the best way to get things moving is to call in a favour when needed.

For this reason, they earn a reputation for 'getting things done' - which can lead to promotion after promotion. While this is undoubtedly good for them - and their pay packets - it can lead to resentment within their teams (who feel that their hard work has been overlooked). To prevent this coming back to bite them later, Pharaohs should take great care to share all credit with their team and acknowledge their contribution. A little recognition and gratitude can go a long way.

Managing a Pharaoh isn't always easy. It's not that they mean to be difficult, it's just that from a very young age, they've come to believe that they're the centre of the Universe - and that it's their way or the highway. This can make them appear bolshy or argumentative to their supervisors - and it's perhaps not surprising that the Pharaohs who haven't yet learned to manage 'upwards' find themselves repeatedly looking for a new job.

PHARAOH: UNDERSTANDING THE SHADOW

In Jungian psychology, the 'shadow' refers to the 'unknown' or unconscious dark side of the personality which the ego does not recognise within itself (even if it's pretty obvious to everyone else!). It could even be said that until we identify and then 'own' our shadow aspect, it'll keep us trapped in self-sabotaging and self-defeating patterns. Just as unpalatably, the 'shadow' is the unowned part of us that manipulates others.

If it's any consolation, we all have a 'shadow'. For the Pharaoh, the shadow plays out through arrogance and hubris. While self belief is a wonderful thing, when it causes someone to be completely blinkered to outside influence, it can lead to disaster further down the road.

Life can sometimes be tough for the Pharaoh because their whole identity is tied up in 'being right'. They can hear others' suggestions as criticisms and they can get into verbal debates in which no one really emerges as the winner. The only way to deal with a Pharaoh who has backed themselves into a corner is to show them a way out in which they're able to **save face**.

Pharaohs can be particularly adept at noticing faults in other people - or mistakes made by them - while easily glossing over their own. This isn't an attribute which others find endearing and goes some way to explaining why people often laugh in glee when a Pharaoh 'trips up' in the public arena. When a Pharaoh is operating from their shadow, the people around them who've suffered through their pomposity and constant demands often delight in them getting their come-uppance - sensing that somehow a magical power has finally meted out some justice!

Sadly, there are some Pharaohs who have managed to develop narcissistic tendencies - using others for their own ends with no respect for their feelings (or for them as human beings). How these behaviours play out varies - but they usually involve some level of cruelty (which is often mental and emotional but can involve physical violence or financial deprivation too).

With their fixed and self-righteous beliefs, Pharaohs can come across as very cold and judgmental and they find no difficulty in airing their disapproval and pointing out other people's flaws. Indeed, they almost feel it to be their duty to pass comment and offer advice - irrespective of whether it was solicited in the first place. However, while Pharaohs can dish it out, they just can't take it themselves. They perceive other people's negative comments as a lack of respect and feel personally affronted.

Shadow Pharaohs can find themselves getting lonelier in old age - especially if their hardened attitudes have caused rifts in their closer relationships. Often they avoid reflecting on how their own behaviours may have caused this state of affairs - and instead 'buy in company' through sycophants and carers so that they don't have to be alone with their thoughts and feelings.

Others seek solace in their money - believing that it offers a level of security that people don't. After all, money doesn't whinge or complain - and nor does it have demands or expectations.

Shadow Pharaohs often use money to control, cajole or threaten - with an inheritance being the weapon of choice. Unsurprisingly, threatening to write people out of a will unless they comply with the Pharaoh's wishes doesn't lead to warm and loving relationships. While Shadow Pharaohs very happily use money in this way, they actually despise other people for being in a position where they can be so controlled - a trap that a Pharaoh will have done all he or she could to avoid throughout their lives. After all, for the Pharaoh, money is power - and they can conceive of nothing worse than being rendered powerless (and thus being a 'nobody' in their own eyes).

The corollary to all this behaviour of course, is that the Shadow Pharaoh fears that people only want to be with them **because of their money**. Often they're right - after all, why else would people put up with being treated so badly? The Pharaoh knows this deep down in their hearts - but rather than being prepared to do the necessary work on themselves, they project their mistrust and anger on to those around them, thus perpetuating the unhappy cycle.

Finally, Shadow Pharaohs stubbornly hold on to the status quo - resisting any change as they fear that it might threaten their power base. The antidote? Lower the mask, see others for who they truly are - and learn to connect with them through the heart.

How the Pharaoh can self-sabotage

Pharaohs often have a seeming inability to see how they may be wrong, even when there is mounting evidence to the contrary. This can ultimately prove both humiliating and costly.

What the Pharaoh deeply believes about themselves

Some deeply-held beliefs are positive while others emanate from the shadows. Intriguingly, these beliefs are often a variation on the same theme:

Light Belief: "Sometimes I struggle too, but I'll never let on, so that you don't have to worry."

Shadow Belief: "Nobody is as good as me, although they'll never admit it."

PHARAOH: HOW THEY APPROACH LIFE

In all relationships, the Pharaoh adopts an approach of expecting everything to be very firmly under their jurisdiction. It's not so much that they feel 'entitled' - although some do - it's more a case of absolute belief in their own sovereignty.

Pharaohs are proud - and wherever they find themselves, they manage to give off an air of authority, as though they travel through life sitting on their regal throne (even if it does only exist in virtual reality). Unsurprisingly, they don't like their authority questioned - and the people around them learn to hone their own diplomatic skills if they're to be 'heard' and 'heeded'.

With their strong sense of allegiance to their 'tribe', Pharaohs often go above and beyond to ensure that those they care about have all they need and desire. They often regard themselves as the lynchpin to everyone's lives and have a strong sense that everything revolves around them.

This can make things a tad difficult for the Pharaoh. Despising weakness, they don't respect people who simply hand their power over and allow themselves to be led without question. However, they're not overly keen on people questioning their authority either. For this reason, Pharaohs can find themselves very much in agreement with the statement that 'it can be lonely at the top'.

Pharaohs can be stubborn - and blind to what they don't know that they don't know. This can, on occasion, give rise to them leading everyone in the wrong direction - and even when this becomes apparent, they find it difficult to backtrack. Saving face is extremely important to the Pharaoh and one of their life lessons is learning at least a degree of humility. If they don't choose to explore this voluntarily, life often has a way of designing circumstances to do the job for them. The adage that 'pride comes before a fall' could have been coined for the Pharaoh.

PHARAOH: AS A ROMANTIC PARTNER

Some people are drawn to having a romantic relationship with the Pharaoh because their every need and desire is catered for - especially in the early days. Similarly, partners are often attracted to Pharaohs because of their power - not necessarily because they're famous, but because life is just so exciting and deliciously far beyond the normal 9-5 of most people. Pharaohs can be wary though and they have an uncanny ability to spot gold-diggers from a mile off. It also has to be said that Pharaohs are not averse to using people who are apparently only after their wealth - but they console themselves that this is a fair exchange. When a Pharaoh loves - and knows that he or she is loved in return for who they *are* (rather than for what they *have*), they often carry on to live 'happily ever after'. Finally, Pharaohs are capable of loving their partners deeply - but make no mistake, they'll love *themselves* every bit as much. And while this can be a good thing in itself, know that noisy rows often ensue when Pharaohs don't get their own way.

Worth considering: Used to ruling the roost, Pharaohs can find it challenging when they partner with people who have equally strong views and opinions. The invitation is for them to cede some control - and to trust their partner to honour their side of the bargain. To their surprise, they often find they rather like it! One area in which Pharaohs particularly struggle is admitting when they get it wrong. Apologising is a complete anathema for them - and in truth, they often find it easier to *show* that they're sorry with a gift.

How the Pharaoh handles money in a relationship

Pharaohs are natural rulers of their dominions - and this includes running the family treasure chest. They take their leadership duties seriously and expect to bankroll pretty much everyone under their jurisdiction. This gives them a sense of power and more than a little 'control', which in turn provides them with a sense of security. While they don't expect thanks per se (after all, 'running things' is their role in life) they do expect to receive *respect* in return.

Integrity is important to the Pharaoh - and they have a strong sense of allegiance to the people around them who they consider to be 'family' (irrespective of whether or not they're related by blood).

PHARAOH: AS A PARENT

Pharaoh parents tend to have very strong ideas about how family life should be - and perhaps unsurprisingly, they see themselves very much as the head of the household. (This can of course, get interesting when there are two Pharaoh parents.) They encourage their children to expand their horizons and often take them on fabulous trips abroad, treat them to meals in the best restaurants and ensure that their offspring feel very at home with all that life has to offer. Pharaoh parents understand the importance of good manners and etiquette and take a great deal of trouble to instil them in their children (or if they don't personally, they'll see to it that the nanny does). Pharaoh parents understand the importance of good schooling - not just for the education itself but also because of the good impression it makes. Oh, and if their children get to rub shoulders with the offspring of well-connected parents, then that can only be helpful as they grow up.

Worth considering: Some Pharaoh parents can actually be quite formidable - running their families with military-style discipline. In order for their children to learn how to handle their own emotions, it's important for their Pharaoh parents to drop their masks on occasion - so that family relationships go deeper than the superficial. While this might make any Pharaoh feel vulnerable at the outset, they should know that everyone benefits (including themselves).

PHARAOH: AS A CHILD

Pharaoh children very happily rule the roost from a young age. Opinionated, talkative and sometimes just plain bossy, Pharaoh children know exactly what they want and don't stop until they get it. They tend to ignore the rules - or at the very least see them as a challenge to be surmounted. They don't always do as well at school as their intelligence would suggest because school somehow feels just that little bit mundane. They can't wait to be grown up when they know they'll have the metaphorical keys to the whole wide world.

Pharaohs don't always go to university - preferring instead to get straight into the world of business and making deals - but those who do opt for further education either find themselves at the top 'big name' universities (otherwise, why bother? Isn't education also about connecting with the future contacts you'll need to build your empire?) or at the famous law and business schools.

Worth considering: Pharaoh children need to be taught to take others' needs and feelings into consideration - and to include and consult (rather than just 'dictate').

PHARAOH: HOW THEY RELATE TO TIME

Pharaohs usually have sufficient time because they're able to pay so many people to help them! From personal assistants through to household help, Pharaohs recognise that 'time is money' so they delegate everything they can to other people, so that they're free to focus solely on what they're best at - overseeing their dominion, developing relationships with other power brokers and making money.

Pharaohs plan in a lot of downtime - after all, don't they deserve it? 'Work hard and play hard' is their motto.

Pharaohs expect punctuality in others - but aren't always so good at arriving for appointments on time themselves. But they remind themselves that what they're doing is *important* - so little matter if someone else has been kept waiting. (Of course, not everyone views the Pharaoh's tardiness in the same way - most especially other Pharaohs, who can't abide the disrespect shown by people who have the temerity to show up late.)

How the Pharaoh breaches boundaries around time

Pharaohs can waste time by getting too much into the 'detail' and micro-managing - rather than 'delegating'.

PHARAOH: HOW THEY DRESS

Clothes are of great importance to the Pharaoh who is prepared to spend over the odds for the right 'look' or 'designer label'. They'll also ensure that their clothes fit properly and they often invest in bespoke tailoring to ensure that wherever they are, they look their best.

Pharaoh's generally do all they can to keep their bodies in shape, so that they cut a good figure. They also have a penchant for youth - and are prepared to do what it takes to look as young as they can. They'll certainly pay for expensive potions, serums and elixirs, and many aren't averse to a little help from cosmetic surgery, or at the very least, Botox and fillers (irrespective of whether they're male or female).

They're also very particular about their hair - and will happily pay a lot to have it cut, coloured and styled (again, this applies to both males and females).

HOW OTHER - HIGH SCORING - 'MONEY TYPES' CAN INFLUENCE THE PHARAOH

Pharaoh - Magician:

This individual is a natural leader and visionary. The Magician introduces an entrepreneurial influence - spotting opportunities and seeing beyond the mundane. Indeed, the Pharaoh-Magician can come up with solutions so quickly that it leaves everyone else astounded.

Watch out for: Armed with bags of natural self-confidence, the Pharaoh-Magician can sometimes adopt a 'my way or the highway' approach that can make others feel distinctly uncomfortable.

Moving forwards: The Pharaoh-Magician should avoid creating enemies by learning to focus on creating a win:win for everyone.

Pharaoh - Joker:

People always enjoy being around this individual as they make life and business fun! Even more importantly, they also recognise that success in business is all about **relationships**. With this combination, the Pharaoh-Joker is a natural leader, host, promoter and salesperson.

Watch out for: This individual needs to understand that the people they're in business with just love it when they're the centre of the Pharaoh-Joker's attention - but can feel rejected and resentful when that attention is directed elsewhere.

Moving forwards: The Pharaoh-Joker needs to recognise the importance of acknowledging others and allowing them to shine.

Pharaoh - Angel:

This individual combines their leadership qualities with their strong desire to make things better for everyone. They're one of the rare people who can not only see the problems facing the world - but who also has the courage to do something about it. They lead where others may fear to tread.

Watch out for: Determined to make the world a better place, the Pharaoh-Angel can sometimes forget about the needs of those closer to home, including themselves.

Moving forwards: The Pharaoh-Angel needs to learn to prioritise themselves and their loved ones - physically and emotionally.

Pharaoh - Architect:

This individual's BIG plans get implemented on time and within budget - and they achieve this by creating a tight framework and measurable action plan for others to follow. They have a very pragmatic and logical approach. Nothing phases them and whatever they set out to achieve, they achieve with flying colours.

Watch out for: The Pharaoh-Architect can come across as very serious, which might be off-putting for some people and downright scary for others. They should recognise that when people are intimidated, they don't perform at their best.

Moving forwards: Great projects are achieved through **people** - and the Pharaoh-Architect needs to learn to nurture their team.

Pharaoh - Prisoner:

This individual is not only able to see what really isn't working, they're also well placed to ensure that things get fixed. Fuelled by a heady mixture of injustice and determination to put 'wrongs' right, they're driven to fight to the end for those causes in which they passionately believe.

Watch out for: Fighting for what seems like a 'worthy cause' can lead to others perceiving the Pharaoh-Prisoner as obsessive, angry or judgemental. Additionally, they can sometimes resolutely remain stuck in their discomfort as they're too haughty to accept outside help.

Moving forwards: The Pharaoh Prisoner needs to learn to keep others on side by inspiring them with a positive vision, after all people are often more inspired by fighting **for** rather than **against** something.

THE MAGICIAN

MAGICIANS have what many consider to be the "Midas" touch – and they're great at creating multiple streams of income. They have a strong entrepreneurial streak and often spot opportunities when others see only problems.

What can help the MAGICIAN: Their ability to see opportunities – even in the unlikeliest of places – means that Magicians have a natural "infectious" optimism which results in people clamouring to work with them. When they understand that some people – especially in their personal life – may want to curb their natural exuberance (in the belief that they're protecting the Magician from disappointment) they begin to understand that other people aren't necessarily being negative, just cautious.

The trap that could undermine the MAGICIAN: While intelligent and persuasive, Magicians often carry their ideas and visions for the future in their heads - failing to communicate them clearly with the people whose help they need to turn their vision into reality. The Magician needs to recognise that he or she can't achieve all that they want to on their own – and that in order for others to be able to help, they first need to understand what the Magician sees.

Three 'Insight Questions' for Magicians:

1. Are you clear in what you want to achieve and have you communicated this clearly to others?

2. Are you focusing your attention and activity in a directed way, or are you scattering your energy in too many directions?

3. Who do you need on the team to help you succeed?

MAGICIAN GLOBAL ROLE: CREATOR

Magicians are self-starting individuals who just love to spot opportunities, solve problems and find better ways to do things. They exist to make the world a better place. While some are artists and others are story tellers, the majority are visionaries and they all have an entrepreneurial spirit. They know - and have always known - that their role is to **create**.

With their highly developed intuition - sometimes even bordering on the psychic - Magicians have an uncanny ability to just **know** what needs to be done. This can be a tough gift for them to handle because they're not always able to explain to those around them how they **know**, they just **know**.

Unsurprisingly, it's all too easy for other people to dismiss their ideas and while Magicians are perfectly capable of putting in the necessary research to prove their inner promptings with logic, they often feel it's a bit of a waste of time and they can quickly become frustrated and irritable.

The problem for many Magicians is that while they see things very clearly, they have trouble believing that what's very obvious to them, isn't actually obvious to everyone around them. Hating being patronised themselves, Magicians tend not to go into lengthy explanations or to provide any rationale for their musings - assuming that others will just 'get it'. Very often they don't. And while they may cover it up well, Magicians can feel very hurt when others seemingly reject their ideas - little realising that actually, the problem is that people just can't keep up with them.

Magicians' minds are always whirring away - spotting a problem and devising a solution almost instantaneously. Of course, their intention isn't to bring every idea to fruition but they love exercising their minds, in much the same way that 'normal' people do crosswords or Sudoko for fun.

Magicians are the philosophers of the world. They seemingly carry a blueprint deep within their hearts of just how the world could be - and with great gusto and a lot of determination they set out to nudge things along with a little of their own particular brand of magic.

Environmentalists, humanitarians and technologists are all powerful expressions of the Magician - set as they are on developing and improving things for everyone and everything on the planet. (And yes, it has to be said that while the vast majority of Magicians have a 'good heart', there are just the occasional few who err into darker realms. Like everyone, Magicians are free to choose their particular path - and intention is everything).

In order to thrive, Magicians need to ensure that everyone's goals are neatly aligned to create a long-term win:win...

But not all Magicians find themselves playing on the world stage. The majority simply create 'worlds' of their own - and develop businesses and consultancies that enable them to pursue the work they love (and get paid at the same time).

While Magicians thrive on having a 'lot on the go' - boredom is their number one enemy - they need to learn to *focus*. Many entrepreneurial types have lots of half-finished projects cluttering up drawers and piled up untidily on their desks - and all of this 'unfinished business' creates a negative vibe. After all, who wants to be constantly reminded of their failures?

With their speed of thought inspiring them, Magicians want to do everything at *once*. Instead, they need to learn to approach things sequentially and to finish one project before embarking on another.

KEY ROLES: Visionary, Strategist, Entrepreneur

KEY BELIEF: "I improve the world with my ideas"

KEY LESSON: Seeing projects through to completion - and beyond

KEY STRENGTH: Imagination

KEY DESIRE: Freedom

MAGICIAN PERSONAL DRIVE: CREATING

Magicians do well to chunk big projects down into bite-sized elements. They thrive on the exhilarating feeling of 'getting lots done' - and feel more energised when they see lots of 'ticks' on their to-do-list rather than just one.

*When Magicians learn to connect their ideas
with the world, their lives transform and become
easy, successful and abundant...*

While appreciating that others are comfortable with goals and action plans, Magicians tend to use their internal operating system to get things done. This can work relatively well for Magicians working on their own, but can cause chaos when they try to work with others.

Great communicators when they're talking with their audience - who are often left inspired and energised by the Magician's vision, they're not so great at sharing the ***finer details*** with their team. Indeed, they often speak in their own kind of shorthand, which they expect everyone else to understand from the outset.

Magicians see their ideas and solutions as a single 'outcome' image in their minds. Achieving this mind-picture seems like a 'no brainer' for a Magician - after all, the image is the map. Unfortunately though, not everyone else sees the same picture (or any picture at all!).

Magicians spend a great deal of time living in their 'inner world' - which can mean that they sometimes miss the niceties of what's going on around them. They might miss birthdays - not because they don't care but simply because it's just not on their inner world 'radar'. They'll appreciate being reminded though, as they never have any intent to hurt or slight - it's just that their minds are often simply on other things.

Magicians love to travel, to explore and to learn about other cultures. They also love to observe how other industries and countries do things, fertilising and cross-pollinating those ideas with their own projects to create something new.

People wonder how Magicians get to have such fertile imaginations - it's relatively simple: they're curious, they observe, they connect ideas, they try things out in their heads. They practice. Constantly. While many believe in the adage that 'Knowledge is power', the Magician knows that 'Knowledge ***applied*** is power' is by far the higher truth.

One of the games Magicians love to play is to work out ways to monetise things. Indeed, they often see money as a game - a means of keeping score.

Unlike some of the other 'Money Types' who can take money very seriously, for the Magician, money is little more than a resource and it's something that they take relatively lightly.

Having said that, Magicians often find that they don't have enough money. It's not that they're not capable of earning it, and it's not that it all slips through their fingers on shiny things - it's just that they're always embarking on new projects which require some level of seed funding. With the sheer volume of new ideas flowing through their hyper-active minds, it's hardly surprising that their imagination often outweighs their ability to keep up financially.

And it's not just money that Magicians complain about - they also struggle with time, for the same reasons. In the same way that shopaholics learn to curb their excesses by setting a 'one in, one out' policy in their wardrobes (every time they buy something they must let go of an existing item), Magicians need to learn that every time they choose to start on a new project, they must knock another one on the head.

For all their visionary prowess, Magicians suffer from one key blindspot. See it, understand it, do something about it - and their lives begin to change as if by magic.

So, what is the blindspot?

The 'instant images' that Magicians have with regard to their ideas are only the first step - not the whole project. To paraphrase multimillionaire copywriter Ted Nicholas, creating the product itself is only 20% of the job done. Eighty percent of your effort needs to go into **promoting** the product.

Yup, that's where the money lies. And yet many Magicians are actually uncomfortable with the very idea of self-promotion. While those with enough money employ others to do it on their behalf, the majority of Magicians have put so much effort into their creation that they have no energy left for promotion. And of course, it's no good having the best product or service in the world if no-one knows about it.

Sadly, once the Magician has recovered from his or her creative exertions, they fall into the trap of believing that their work must have been 'no good' - or the world would have been beating a path to their door.

Rather than stop to consider that nobody actually knows about their work, they instead devote themselves to an exciting *new* project. After all, Magicians love nothing more than creating - it makes them feel that they're living 'on purpose'.

MAGICIAN: RELATIONSHIP WITH MONEY

In some ways, Magicians can be a little naive - or maybe they're just 'business romantics'. They can spend considerable time in enjoyable reveries about how much the world will appreciate their creative efforts when they 'make it big'- but they need to wake up to the fact that day dreaming about how they're going to **connect their ideas with the world** would be a much more profitable use of their time.

Wise Magicians find people to partner with who can help them promote their ideas within the marketplace (in 'Money Types' language, that would be the Joker) - leaving them free to do what they do best: create.

Enlightened Magicians however, choose to bring in a third player (and in Money Types language, that would be the Architect) - who's love of organising and seeing things through to fruition completes this powerful triangle.

> *Magicians know that however tough life gets,*
> *they can rely on their creativity and imagination*
> *to guide themselves - and the people around*
> *them - to a better future.*

Magicians love to have a variety of income streams - and they usually have lots of money making ideas on the go. In time, Magicians come to learn that making money is much more fun - and much easier - when they have their living expenses covered. In the olden days, people like Leonardo da Vinci would have had a patron (someone who provided them with a decent roof over their heads and who organised things like food and entertainment. All someone like Leonardo needed to do was create!)

Nowadays, such patronage is less forthcoming, so modern era Magicians need to create their own 'cash cow'. Some do this with their own business or consultancy which pays a retainer, others do it with a job.

While Magicians don't necessarily understand the value they bring to an employer, they do want their time to generate as much cash as possible - after all, they'll need it to seed fund their personal projects. For this reason, they're usually able to put forward a fairly persuasive argument when it comes to negotiating their pay package.

Ideal careers for Magicians

Futurist | Media | Inventor | Design | Diplomacy

Product Design | Strategy | Writer | Speaker | Artist

Changes in the law - especially with regard to financial matters - usually escape the Magician, who rarely has his or her finger on the pulse of what's happening in the world of finance. Missing the opportunities offered by workplace pension schemes for example - even dismissing such things as irrelevant - can be costly in terms of losing out on what is effectively free money (taking into account employer contributions and tax relief offered by the government).

Often quite comfortable with risk, Magicians are self-determining individuals who like to make their lives as interesting as possible. When they eventually figure out how to make money flow, they may be surprised by just **how much** comes their way. And when it does, they're generally very comfortable with the idea of paying specialists to look after and grow their money for them.

In his world famous book "*The 7 Habits of Highly Effective People*", Stephen Covey writes a whole chapter about 'Beginning with the End in Mind" - something that Magicians would do well to heed.

Magicians always have lots of *ideas* when it comes to making money - and with their boundless energy and creative spirit, they know that if one idea doesn't work, they can simply turn their attention to the next one. The trick though, is making sure that they're not swept off their feet by every new 'bright and shiny' concept - after all, when it comes to making money, seeing the job through to the **outcome** is where the serious wealth lies.

While the Magician may spend their early years working for someone else (either in a smaller business or for a much larger corporation) - they'll come to look back on this time as their unofficial apprenticeship. If they're honest, they'll probably struggle with other people's rules and frameworks when frankly, they just can't help but think of a better way of doing it themselves.

But they do well to stick with it - as there's a lot of merit in being able to learn from other people's mistakes. Additionally, there's a kind of 'maturing' or 'polishing' that occurs when we have no choice but to adapt to the hurly burly of other people and **their** agendas (and we also get to learn a lot too, from their **hidden** agendas). Magician entrepreneurs who have never worked for anyone else (and this most often applies in family-owned businesses) just don't know what they don't know - and this can be expensively dangerous.

The Magician is a lifelong learner with bags of energy...

Having said all that, from the outset, the Magician knows deep down that they're going to end up working for themselves. They probably also know that it won't be long before they're rendered completely 'unemployable'. They gain so much experience so quickly - lifelong learners that they are - that they'll simply terrify any potential future employers with their speed of thought, their fierce sense of independence and their boundless energy.

Investing in themselves - particularly in terms of their own personal and business development is their winning strategy and they're not afraid to bootstrap their ideas. Indeed, being under-capitalised is often the nature of their game. Partly it's exciting. Partly it's because they enjoy the thrill of creating. Partly it's because they simply don't know any other way.

It was Albert Einstein who described the definition of insanity as doing the same thing over and over again, hoping for a different result. While it may now have become a bit of a cliche, it's still a maxim that's good for Magicians - as it pays them to take stock every so often to work out what is, and what isn't, working.

At some point in their lives, Magicians wonder whether they should attempt to find a way to clone themselves, so that they can get even more done. But actually, this would just double their problems. What they really need is to collaborate with others who have **different** strengths. Often for those Magicians running their own show, what they really need is a Joker to connect their ideas with the world and an Architect to build some much needed systems and processes.

When the Magician begins collaborating in this way with others, they soon find a positive shift in their fortunes. As we've already seen, the dream team is the Joker to make the sales - and the Architect to oversee implementation. Yes, the Architect may make things feel like they're no longer quite so much **fun**, but then when the money starts rolling in, the Magician comes to deeply appreciate this new found **success**.

And when the coffers start to build, that's the time that the savvy Magician begins to make investments in something **other** than themselves. Shares, property, pensions - all the stuff that may not immediately light their fire - can however, help the Magician to build the serious wealth their creativity deserves. They, more than many, appreciate the power of compound interest over time. Channelling their earnings into more traditional investment vehicles does at least go some way to mitigating the Magician's tendency to keep ploughing money into their own pet projects. Of course, there's nothing to say that they can't do both - but if they want a calm family life, the Magician shouldn't keep betting their family home on their own entrepreneurial whims and ventures.

How to have difficult money conversations at home

Generally more comfortable with ideas, the Magician tends to see conversations about money as an annoying, stressful **obstacle** that prevents them from getting on with much more interesting things.

The best approach with a Magician is to remind them that when it comes to money, their entrepreneurial perspective and creativity is really **needed**. After all, Magicians who are free of money worries are always more successful in the long term because they're operating from a freer mental and emotional space - unencumbered by subconscious worries that can weigh them down.

When it comes to talking about money in business

The Magician is fairly comfortable talking about money in business - mainly because they see it merely as the 'fuel' for bringing their projects to life. However, people operating from their Shadow Magician have a dangerous tendency to over-extend themselves - believing that somehow they'll manage to pull the 'white rabbit out of the hat' when it's time to pay the bills. This shadow side can also play out with the Magician having too many projects on the go at the same time - resulting in none of them growing to the point where they generate money. This can lead to frustration - and irritation - whenever the subject of money is brought up.

The Magician's attitude to financial risk

More than anyone or anything else, Magicians back *themselves* - and they are among the most likely to ultimately have 'wealth' based on the businesses they've built. With success under their belt, they then enjoy the idea of using their money to make more money, which is why they're more likely to be involved with investments from mid-life onwards. As well as being generally comfortable with risk because they recognise that change brings opportunity, they're used to taking personal responsibility in life, so Magicians tend not to be inclined to fret or blame their investment management team when markets fall.

How to persuade or sell to the Magician

The Magician likes their ideas to be *heard* - and they blossom when encouraged. They thrive on feeling understood and will happily pay people who can monetise their best concepts. While they're not micromanagers, Magicians don't want to let go of the reins completely - after all, this is their baby.

When presenting to them, know that any printed literature needs to be brief. Easy-to-assimilate infographics are perfect.

MAGICIANS AT WORK: As the boss

Magician bosses are fun to be around and life is never boring. With their big ideas, futuristic outlook and endless search for new opportunities, everyone working alongside the Magician can expect to be stimulated and challenged.

When it comes to gathering a team together, Magicians can fall into the trap of recruiting people 'in their own image'. We all naturally gravitate towards people who are like us - and Magicians love nothing more than discussing ideas and talking 'concepts'. But who they really need on their team are planners and organisers.

Above all, Magician bosses need people around them who 'get it' quickly (especially when the Magician is communicating in their own peculiar shorthand that generally speaking, only they can understand) and who are able to convert general ideas into specific plans and completed outcomes.

Similarly, Magician bosses can unnerve their teams by jumping on every new 'good idea' - leaving other projects for dust. This can lead to people feeling demoralised - why bother working late and being really committed if your boss is only going to change their mind about everything a bit later on? When this happens, and sadly it does all too often, people simply stop trying so hard and output slows - much to the frustration of the Magician who is still galloping away (even if only in circles).

One of the most powerful antidotes to their mad-professor approach is for a Magician boss to hire a PA who can clean up behind them and coordinate things moving forward.

Magician bosses are always very open to ideas and better ways of doing things. Others however can find them flaky and accuse them of being unable to make a decision and stick to it. The Magician just can't understand this mode of thinking - why would you continue down a particular path when you'd subsequently discovered that there was a better way?

Magicians can often be good at creating systems and processes for other people - but they're less adept at following them. It's not arrogance that's at the root of the problem - but repetition. Magicians just hate repeating things - whether it's repeating what they've just said, repeating what they're doing or repeating mistakes. And if a mistake does occur, Magician bosses don't tend to conduct a witch hunt to discover **who** was responsible. They'd rather work out **what** went wrong - and create a workaround to ensure that it can never happen again.

As managers & colleagues

Magicians are creative - and their levels of energy, enthusiasm and sheer output can astonish those around them. They tend to work best when they have responsibility for their own work.

That is of course, assuming that the Magician is **engaged** in what they're doing. If they're bored, or if their work involves any repetition, they can become all too easily distracted. Occasionally, they'll just waste time - more often, they'll spend a lot of effort trying to work out how things could be improved, rather than just getting on with the job in hand.

But their need for 'continuous improvement' shouldn't be overlooked - indeed it should be encouraged (just not when there's a deadline looming). Magicians are often great at finding faster ways of doing things which can save money - or suggesting other ways in which products or services can be adapted, which can generate extra income and improve profitability. Challenge a Magician to come up with ways to bring in extra income to a business and they'll fly! Yes, they'll love the recognition and the responsibility - but more than anything else, they simply love the game of making money. (Reward them - and they'll do it again and again).

Friendly, interesting and knowledgable, Magicians are good people to have around and they'll play their part in keeping morale up. (Annoy them and dismiss their ideas and you'll find it can be a completely different story. Unhappy Magicians can waste a lot of time moaning and complaining with their colleagues - little realising the impact they're having. But the good news is that they're naturally forgiving and let bygones-be-bygones.)

Magicians are good at seeing the big picture but can sometimes struggle to work out each single step required to bring the overall vision into reality. This can lead to them giving poor instructions to their team, who can become frustrated when they find themselves having to re-do some of their work because they weren't properly instructed in the first place.

Magicians can be mercurial - up one minute and down the next. To onlookers, Magicians seem to thrive on chaos. It is true, they do. Don't expect a Magician to have a tidy desk for long.

MAGICIANS: UNDERSTANDING THE SHADOW

In Jungian psychology, the 'shadow' refers to the 'unknown' or unconscious dark side of the personality which the ego does not recognise within itself (even if it's pretty obvious to everyone else!). It could even be said that until we identify and then 'own' our shadow aspect, it'll keep us trapped in self-sabotaging and self-defeating patterns. Just as unpalatably, the 'shadow' is the unowned part of us that manipulates others.

If it's any consolation, we all have a 'shadow'. For the Magician, the shadow plays out through self-doubt and avoidance of feelings. While they're great at understanding the **world** around them - and seeing a myriad of possibilities for improvement - they don't always get it right when it comes to understanding their relationships with other **people**.

And it's often the emotional aspects of relationships that can cause havoc for Magicians - who tend to feel safer in the world of the intellect, rather than the nebulous world of emotions.

Indeed, when there's emotional 'stuff' going on, they can find it very hard to determine what's 'their's' and what actually belongs to other people. For this reason, Magicians can find themselves absorbing other people's emotions, without realising.

Sooner rather than later, the Magician often finds themselves displaying those very same emotions - perhaps anger or sadness - but with no understanding why. Feeling bewildered and out of control, they quickly choose to divert their minds to another **idea**, which seems both safer and well, just more fun.

This lack of emotional understanding often first arose when Magicians were denied the right to 'feel their feelings' when they were children - often by parents who had limited emotional intelligence themselves. Parents who were uncomfortable with their own emotions simply swallowed, denied or projected them onto their own children - who simply didn't have the tools to understand or protect themselves. As they grow up, this can leave them in danger of seeing relationships through distorted lenses. Having learned to swallow down any uncomfortable or turbulent emotions, they find it difficult to discern what's true and what's not in terms of how they - and the people around them - are **truly feeling**.

And for those Magicians who struggle to understand and see their own self-worth, they can mistakenly assume that they are somehow the **cause** of other people's negative emotions. This can lead to much distress and soul searching. Indeed, it can be their Achilles heel - as much time and energy that could have been devoted to their creations is instead diverted to trying to understand their inner jangled nerves.

As in the workplace, Magicians don't seek to apportion blame - rather, they know that when they can finally **understand**, they'll be free. For this reason, many Magicians find themselves interested in various types of personal development.

Finally, some Magicians - again perhaps in an unwitting throwback to their childhoods - learned that simply 'shutting down' rather than sharing their ideas - was the safest option because their families and teachers just simply didn't seem to 'get them'. Magicians often have such a broad intuitive understanding about so many different things that their 'elders' can fall into the trap of mistaking their innate cleverness for 'showing off' or 'grandiosity'. But in truth, the Magicians were simply trying to learn, explore and grow. However, when people seemed cross with them, rather than recognising that the root of the problem didn't actually lie with them, they took what seemed like the easier option, and learned to keep quiet to restore the peace.

Given their propensity to live inside their 'heads', it's no wonder that Magicians don't always communicate well with the people around them. Having said that, they have no difficulty whatsoever when it comes to sharing their BIG ideas. It's the smaller details and articulating exactly what's required that can all too easily trip up the Magician.

While Magicians enjoy 'talking things through', they can get easily distracted - with the result that instructions and requests can get horribly mangled. For this reason, it's often best - for everyone - if the Magician writes their instructions down. This way, they can hone and revise their remarks on 'their own time', rather than wasting everyone else's.

When misunderstandings occur - and they do - Magicians can get twitchy and tetchy. They hate not being able to make themselves understood.

This can result in people choosing to keep their own counsel rather than admit to not understanding what the Magician in their midst actually wants - which leads to yet further confusion and irritation. A vicious circle ensues and Magicians can end up feeling that it would simply be easier to 'do everything themselves'. Of course, this isn't true. Collaboration is the name of the game when it comes to success - and all that's truly needed is for the Magician to slow down, focus and learn to feel comfortable sharing their thoughts and plans.

How the Magician can self-sabotage

The Magician is sadly often unable to admit (especially to themselves) that one of their precious creations just isn't going to succeed - with the result that the pain continues for much longer than necessary.

What the Magician deeply believes about themselves

Some deeply-held beliefs are positive while others emanate from the shadows. Intriguingly, these beliefs are often a variation on the same theme:

Light Belief: "Solving problems and creating opportunities out of thin air isn't work, it's fun!"

Shadow Belief: "I hide behind my creativity."

MAGICIANS: HOW THEY APPROACH LIFE

In all conceptual relationships, curious, enthusiastic and creative Magicians have learned from the outset to expand their boundaries - and they love nothing more than exploring and experiencing everything that life has to offer. But as we've just seen, it can be a rather different story when it comes to more complicated inter-personal emotional relationships.

Magicians hate repetition and boredom and naturally gravitate to what's novel and exciting. They're early adopters - and they see life as an exciting voyage of discovery. They love delving into a wide array of seemingly disparate subjects - and then 'connecting the dots' in original ways which can lead to new theories that advance human kind or to new ways of creating art or making music.

Magicians enjoy the process of being alive - there's just so much to learn and experience - and they spend every moment with almost breathless enthusiasm. Unless they're bored, in which case they can waste hours and hours ruminating on nothing in particular, with very little to show for it in the end.

Magicians enjoy learning about new cultures and different ways of doing things. They love travel for this reason - and there's little they enjoy more than discussing the problems and solutions of the world with a wide variety of people.

Given their fascination with people, Magicians tend to be all-embracing by nature - seeing everyone as worthy of respect, irrespective of their position in life. While they accept that total equality just isn't possible - they do carry a strong belief that there should be equality of 'opportunity'.

Finally, Magicians have a kaleidoscopic perspective on life. It's what keeps them interesting and interested.

MAGICIAN: AS A ROMANTIC PARTNER

Magicians can be wonderfully romantic - and are very capable of creating the kind of memories that last a lifetime. With their unusual take on life and constantly shifting perspective, Magicians always make life interesting. They treat everyone around them as their equal and don't stand on ceremony - and while they're not demanding in terms of expecting people to **do** things **for** them, they absolutely love it when their creative work is appreciated. Visionaries that they are, Magicians tend to have exciting plans - whether that's for the home, holidays or how to bring money in to the household. They're encouraged by their partner's enthusiasm and can achieve great things. Conversely, if a spouse or partner repeatedly throws cold water on their ideas, they'll eventually shut down. While they get the need for planning, Magicians aren't great at the detail - and it's good if they can either have their spouse 'keep the books', or pay someone else to do so.

Worth considering: Birthing their creative ideas - and finding ways to monetise them, is a constant preoccupation for Magicians who have such belief in what's possible that they're totally prepared to back themselves. Indeed, they're in their power when they back themselves and don't have to answer to anyone else. Having said that, Magicians think nothing of re-mortgaging their home or using savings - earmarked for the *future* - to fund something they're creating *now*. Of course, other people aren't always as prepared to endanger their future 'security' - which can lead to misunderstandings, distrust and arguments.

How the Magician handles money in a relationship

If they're understood and supported, Magicians can be great providers. However, they tend to dislike the idea of budgeting - not because they don't agree with it per se, it's just that they've got lots of other things to do (and anyway, reality never seems to match a pre-planned budget, so why bother?). Magicians without access to money feel stifled - and a stifled Magician isn't fun to be around. The Magician's desire to get their new projects off the ground *now* make them good targets for banks and credit companies - and sadly, they are capable of racking up considerable debt (with or without their partner's knowledge). While they think about the future - a lot - such is the Magician's self-belief, they *know* they can make everything come good in the end. Usually they're right (once they've done some work on themselves) but occasionally things can go wrong. Badly wrong. But, Magicians are self-starters, so after a little self-recrimination, they'll pick themselves up and start again. And often, they'll persevere until they achieve the prize that they always knew was their's from the outset.

MAGICIAN: AS A PARENT

Magicians take parenting seriously - but lightly. They encourage their children to learn, to explore and to test their boundaries. Magicians' households are often noisy - full of conversation, debate and discussion. Their children are encouraged to read - and Magicians tend to give home to copious books and magazines on a wide variety of topics. Magicians ensure their children have everything they need - from a roof over their heads to food on the table. They also allocate funds to expanding their offspring's horizons - whether that's through visits to local museums and art galleries or further afield to explore different cultures and landscapes. Magicians love to educate their children but are less inclined to spend on fashion or fads. (But they're secretly delighted when their children work out ways to make the money they need to buy the things they want!). Magicians also love to spend creative time with their children - and provide them with all the tools they need to paint, craft, cook and make music. The children of Magicians who are busy in their businesses can sometimes feel overlooked but this too, contributes to their learning as they learn to amuse themselves, exercise their imaginations and become self-sufficient.

Worth considering: While children need some boundaries and rules, they truly blossom when their unique gifts are recognised, developed and appreciated.

MAGICIAN: AS A CHILD

Magician children are often 'older than their years' - possibly because they spend so much time reading, learning and having in-depth conversations with adults. Less good at learning by rote (like their Magician elders, they find repetition tedious) they fare much better at school and beyond, when they get to apply their knowledge and intelligence to their subjects. They love debate and writing essays. They also love learning for the sake of it - although they sometimes struggle to see the point of exams. Magician children have no problem stretching their comfort zones and sometimes it can be difficult to rein them in. They can be dismissive of pointless rules and can get into trouble for not towing the line at school, although they do tend to stay on the right side of the law. (The very idea of losing their freedom is enough to keep them out of serious trouble.) Magician children may put a little aside in their piggy-banks - but they'd much rather be industrious and earn money through a variety of endeavours.

Worth considering: Magician children need to know that they're loved for *who* they are - and not just for what they *know* and *do*.

MAGICIAN: HOW THEY RELATE TO TIME

Magicians never have enough time - there's always so much more that they could be doing. They also suffer from the fact that 'doing things in their head' is almost instantaneous whereas having to do the same thing in reality can feel laboriously slow. Worse, Magicians feel that they've already done the job once - in their imagination - and that doing it again in 'real time' is just mere repetition. And Magicians hate repetition, which may go part of the way to explain why they don't always get their projects finished and shipped! Magicians love it when other people are punctual - seeing it as a sign of respect, but while they do their best to be punctual themselves, they don't always succeed. Whenever they plan for a journey they usually anticipate the possibility of a delay, but on the day, they still fail to allow sufficient contingency time.

How the Magician breaches boundaries around time

Magicians love discussing ideas and embarking on shiny new projects. However, they can waste time and energy by not fully pulling the plug on projects which were once started - but never completed. This causes a subtle energy 'drain' - rather like a computer crashing or operating sub-optimally because too many programmes are running at the same time.

MAGICIAN: HOW THEY DRESS

Magicians can be flamboyant, colourful and gorgeously dressed - or, if they're exercising their minds on a really big project or creation, they can look as though they've been dragged through the proverbial hedge backwards. Magicians are attracted to the unusual and they're never slavish followers of fashion. Instead, they'll wear unusual combinations or they'll make an ensemble completely their own by adding in some accessories they've bought from an exotic excursion. Ostentatious displays of wealth don't really do it for Magicians, although they can reward themselves with something just a little bit flashy if they feel that their hard work paid off and that they deserve it.

HOW OTHER - HIGH SCORING - 'MONEY TYPES' CAN INFLUENCE THE MAGICIAN

Magician - Pharaoh:

As a natural visionary and leader, this individual is able to lead and inspire a team to achieve great things. Using their ability to spot entrepreneurial opportunities, the Magician-Pharaoh has the deep inner confidence that few others rarely get to enjoy.

Watch out for: A self-confident quick thinker, the Magician-Pharaoh can be brusque and impatient with people who can't keep up. Worse, they can be arrogant and let past successes blind them to the truth of what's happening now. Trample on too many people on the way, and there will be delight and jubilation when the Magician-Pharaoh suffers a set-back.

Moving forwards: The Magician-Pharaoh should avoid creating enemies by learning to focus on creating a win:win for everyone.

Magician - Joker:

People always enjoy being around this individual as they make business fun. Even more importantly, the Magician-Joker also recognises that success in business is all about relationships. A natural visionary, host, promotor and salesperson, this individual creates remarkable scenarios and unique solutions - all cleverly designed to make everyone around them feel special and delighted - which means that they benefit from a positive reputation. People will often recommend and refer clients to this individual.

Watch out for: This individual needs to understand that the people they're in business with just love it when they're the centre of the Magician-Joker's attention - but can feel rejected and resentful when that attention is directed elsewhere.

Moving forwards: The Magician-Joker needs to recognise the importance of acknowledging others and allowing them to shine.

Magician - Angel:

This individual combines their entrepreneurial qualities with their desire to make things better for everyone. They're one of the rare people who can see the problems facing the world - and have the vision to do something about it. They lead where others may fear to tread.

Watch out for: Determined to make the world a better place, the Magician-Angel can sometimes forget about the needs of those closer to home, including themselves.

Moving forwards: The Magician-Angel needs to learn to prioritise themselves and their loved ones - physically and emotionally.

Magician - Architect:

This individual's BIG vision gets implemented - on time and within budget - and they achieve this by creating a tight framework and measurable action plan for others to follow. People with this combination often run seriously successful organisations. They have a very pragmatic and logical approach. Nothing phases them and whatever they set out to achieve, they achieve with flying colours!

Watch out for: High on intellect and lower on emotional savvy, the Magician-Architect can come across as very serious - which might be off-putting for some people and down right scary for others. They need to recognise that when people are intimidated, they don't perform at their best.

Moving forwards: The Magician-Architect needs to understand that great projects are achieved through ***people*** - and learn to nurture them.

Magician - Prisoner:

With this combination, the Magician-Prisoner is able to see what *isn't* working and what most definitely needs to be fixed. Fuelled by a heady mixture of injustice and determination to put 'wrongs' right, this individual can be driven to fight to the bitter end for those causes in which they passionately believe.

Watch out for: Fighting for what seems like a 'worthy cause' can lead to others perceiving the Magician-Prisoner as obsessive, angry or judgmental. Additionally, they can over-think, especially when it comes to working out how things might go *wrong*.

Moving forwards: The Magician-Prisoner needs to learn to keep others on-side by inspiring them with a positive vision - and remember that people are more inclined to want to fight *for* - rather than *against* - something.

THE JOKER

JOKERS know only too well that life is for living – NOW! With their fun loving outlook, easy-to-get-on-with attitude and all round zest for life, it's hardly surprising that people naturally gravitate towards them. What also makes Jokers attractive is their generosity – and as they often say, "You can't take it with you".

What can help the JOKER: Their fun-loving, easy-going nature means they'll never be short of company – or opportunities. People love having the Joker in 'their gang' - and their 'live in the moment' attitude gives Jokers a particular aptitude for sales roles, where they can build a relationship quickly, do the deal and then move straight on to the next adventure.

The trap that could undermine the JOKER: Jokers can become easily bored and distracted, which means they're inclined to start many more projects than they're ever likely to finish. They can get around this by creating an overall - exciting - vision for the rest of their lives and using meaningful goals as stepping stones to help them keep on track.

Three 'Insight Questions' for Jokers:

1. What do you need to plan and action today to ensure that you continue to live the life you want in the future?

2. Are you using some of the money you could be using for your own future to pay for other people's 'fun' (which means that they get to save for their future, at your expense)?

3. What do you really enjoy in life, and how can you use it to make money?

JOKER GLOBAL ROLE: CELEBRATOR OF LIFE

Jokers are fun-loving individuals who bring colour and joy to life and who thrive on relationships. They know - and have always known - that their role is to connect people to people and people to ideas.

Less inclined to dredge deep enough to come up with their own creative solutions to the world's problems, they nevertheless recognise a good idea when they see one and love nothing more than 'getting it out there'.

Armed with natural social skills and able to have a friendly conversation with just about anyone, Jokers start building their 'little black book' of contacts from a very young age. Their crowd simply grows bigger and bigger as they get older.

Gifted with the ability to tell a good story and to make other people laugh, Jokers are usually highly popular and find themselves invited to a wide variety of social gatherings - both of a private nature and for business.

They're enthusiastic networkers, delightfully persuasive and are the world's most natural salespeople. People enjoy listening to them and want to hang out with them - after all, wherever the Joker is, there's a good time to be had!

Fearless, excited by life and exuberant by nature, Jokers don't enjoy situations that demand they play by the rules.

With an inherent belief that rules are made to be broken - or at least tested and bent - Jokers can have a disregard for both their own safety and other people's boundaries.

Broken limbs, points on their licence for driving at excessive speeds and even a spell in rehab are all distinct possibilities for hardened Jokers - who love nothing more than pushing their limits. Fast cars and motor bikes appeal - as do physically demanding and testing sports.

Anything that's guaranteed to provide a thrill is catnip to Jokers and they love to experiment and try everything out. Blessed with active imaginations, they'll backpack to exotic places, test their taste buds with unusual foods and possibly even dabble with drugs in order to see what it's like to 'get out of their mind'!

Jokers don't always have the lengthiest of attention spans which can be frustrating for all those around them. Bored Joker children play up their teachers and parents, bored Joker adults do as little as they can get away with, much to the chagrin of their employers.

In order to thrive, Jokers need to ensure that everyone's goals are neatly aligned and learn how to win over the hearts and minds of everyone, including their bosses.

However, happily, there is a very easy-to-apply antidote. Simply show the Joker what prizes they could earn for seeing a project through to its conclusion and they'll soon play ball. Offer exciting prizes that are unusual and unobtainable in any other way - and the Joker will excel.

Jokers like to shine and be seen. If they can achieve this through personal excellence, then they will. A Joker salesperson (and the best ones are) who's inspired by the top prize on offer will leave their colleagues for dust and they'll hit the top of the leader board time and time again. But when greedy or jealous business owners fall into the trap of capping what they can earn, the Joker will quickly become demoralised and their sales results will slump. Unless this is quickly rectified, the Joker can find themselves fired for 'not hitting targets' - much to their bewilderment. This can lead to the Joker losing confidence in themselves (rather than seeing that it was a stupid system that let them down).

KEY ROLES: Ambassador, Connector, Communicator

KEY BELIEF: "I bring the joy into life"

KEY LESSON: Planning for tomorrow while living for today

KEY STRENGTH: Gratitude

KEY DESIRE: Fun

JOKER PERSONAL DRIVE: HAVING FUN

Jokers hate being controlled or told what to do, and when presented with a 'dare', they're likely to accept with alacrity - keen to test their mettle. They love being egged on by their friends and colleagues and from a young age, they've learned that the most effective way to be accepted by the 'group' is by playing the clown. (The fact that this can lead to poor grades further down the line is of absolutely no concern to the young Joker - although their parents may have sleepless nights.)

A Joker's self-belief is one of his or her strongest assets. People managing them need to recognise this - but colleagues and supervisors can mistake their natural optimism and exuberance for cockiness and arrogance. This can be further exacerbated by the Joker's lack of deference to hierarchical niceties - which disgruntled bosses can interpret as disrespect. Turf wars can break out.

When Jokers serve others as well as themselves, their lives truly begin to blossom...

Jokers are very comfortable with emotion - and express it freely. They find it hard to connect with their more buttoned-up counterparts who they can dismiss as rigid, serious and even worse, boring. When Jokers have something to celebrate, everyone gets invited to join in. Equally, if something has upset or annoyed a Joker, everyone will know about it. Emotions pass through Jokers very quickly however - and any bad spell will soon be replaced with their naturally sunny outlook. Natural optimists, Jokers are the charmers, mediators and diplomats of all the 'Money Types' - and as such, they can get away with a lot. They're also great story tellers and often use the medium of narrative (especially if there's a comedic angle) to reveal wisdom and truth in such a way that they can be 'heard'. Enlightened Jokers descend from the court jesters of old, who'd give guidance to their sovereigns in a way that no other courtier would dare.

Finally, Jokers find a way to dance through life - and are often surrounded by people who'll help them celebrate. The smart ones also quietly put a little aside for their future - recognising that life with no money simply isn't...well, fun!

JOKER: RELATIONSHIP WITH MONEY

Rarely savers from a very young age, Jokers have a lot to learn when it comes to money. Often their innate ability to **make** money clouds their judgement when it comes to the **value** of money. For them, it's often a case of 'easy come, easy go' and the Joker often skips through life believing that there's 'plenty more where that came from'. And so there is, if they're prepared to work for it. However, if they're not careful, they could end up having to work while others are luxuriating in the joys of retirement - simply because they didn't plan well enough for their future.

Lucky Jokers will have had parents who repeatedly drilled into them the necessity of putting money aside 'now', to take take care of 'later'. How they'll have hated those boring parental monologues, rolling their eyes at the sheer dreariness of it all.

More than all the rest of the 'Money Types', Jokers lack the capacity to believe that tomorrow will ever come. Often youthful and always retaining their sense of adventure, Jokers simply can't believe that they'll grow old. A few prefer the rock and roll idea of dying young, the rest just never stop to consider it. But Jokers who have to carry on working to pay the bills when their retired friends are off having fun will very quickly get resentful. They won't remember all the fun they've had themselves in the past...instead, they'll just think that life has dealt them a particularly bad hand now.

Jokers love freedom and abhor routine. And they love having money in their pockets. Some will be tempted to run their own business - and at first, they're likely to do well, whatever their industry.

Why? Because with their natural sales skills, they'll quickly find fee-paying customers and clients. However, their singular lack of prowess when it comes to the boring things of life, like keeping records, filing accounts and following procedures will soon dampen their ardour.

If the Joker can quickly find an office manager to take all this drudgery away from them, then their business is likely to thrive. Without it, they'll become despondent, lose their sparkle and become dismayed when their clients walk away disappointed at the lack of customer service and follow-up they've received. Jokers running businesses can even become so buried in paperwork that they give up, with a few even turning to the bottle. Unsurprisingly, these Jokers' businesses don't survive.

The Jokers who do the best are those who recognise that they should be focusing on creating 'passive income' (usually through property, investments or other people working for them).

When they're able to generate (and maintain) more monthly passive income than their monthly expenses, then the Joker has hit the jackpot. Now they don't have to work for anyone else ever again. Now they've bought their own freedom. Now they can be satisfied that they've proven their worth (even if only to themselves).

Additionally, having multiple income streams provides plenty of variety for the Joker - and even more interestingly, they can run these side-line enterprises with other people (particularly a spouse), and what could be more fun than that?

When a business milestone is achieved, Jokers celebrate. In fact, Jokers find it pretty easy to celebrate most things - and there needs to be room in their own personal expense account to accommodate ad-hoc expenditure. However, once they're free of fixed employment, Jokers are pretty adept at turning their hand to whatever it takes to bring in a few extra wads of cash as and when they need it.

Jokers come to discover that relationships provide the stage from which they can share their boundless joy, enthusiasm and influence with the world.

Often acting on impulse - that's what keeps the fun flowing in their lives - Jokers would be the first to admit that they're just not great at 'going without' in the present. They're also not risk averse when it comes to buying things on the 'never, never' - but they need to keep a watchful eye on this before they become choked with debt. (They also need to bear in mind that Jokers are notorious for burying their heads in the sand when things get difficult.)

And when Jokers learn to think about things in terms of 'spending', 'investing' and 'saving', the light bulb starts to burn very brightly indeed.

Understanding their own value and loving nothing more than negotiating a great deal, Jokers can often end up earning more than their peers.

Jokers don't leave anything to chance when it comes to remuneration - knowing that more money means more fun!

Ideal careers for Jokers

Sales | Diplomacy | Mediation | Teaching | Speaking

Comedy | Music | Theatre | Media | Interior Design

Property | Fashion | Travel | Hospitality

It has to be said though, that changes in the law - especially with regard to financial matters - often completely escape the Joker, who rarely has his or her finger on the pulse of what's happening in the world of finance. Jokers often miss the opportunities offered by workplace pension schemes for example - even dismissing such things as irrelevant. A wise Joker recognises that every single advantage (however small) adds to incremental growth, which can make a considerable difference in the long run.

Often quite comfortable with risk, Jokers are self-determining individuals who like to make their lives as stress-free as possible. For this reason, they rather like the idea of paying specialists to look after and grow their money for them.

In his world famous book *"The 7 Habits of Highly Effective People"*, Stephen Covey writes a whole chapter about "Beginning with the End in Mind" - something that Jokers would do well to heed.

With their inherently sunny nature, people gravitate towards the Joker. Wonderfully, their lives are often made easier by the people around them - who loving helping out and paving the Joker's path to **success**.

Many describe the Joker as naturally lucky - and some might even be a tad jealous of the ease with which these individuals seem to dance through life. Clever Joker - they've worked out that the **only** way to make money is through people - through their contacts, their connections and their network. And hey, for them it's all an absolute hoot to boot!

They've also discovered that when they're in flow with money, their confidence to attract more of it just grows and grows. On one hand this is great - but on the other, the cash can start growing a hole in the Joker's pocket and they can find themselves wasting it on feel-good toys and hedonistic pleasures.

With this approach though, the Joker slowly begins to find that their easy relationship with money starts to turn into boredom and disrespect.   It's all just 'too easy'. Hardly surprising then that at this point, the Joker starts to throw in a little self-sabotage, just to keep things interesting.

The solution?

There are in fact two solutions - and happily for the Joker, they're not mutually exclusive.

The first is to buddy up with an entrepreneurial, creative Magician. Sharing and selling the Magician's ideas to the world is a pleasurable and easy path to making money for the Joker - who can very happily **earn a lot** from the process!

When the Joker learns to collaborate with others, they discover the fastest way to amass their fortune. Along with the Magician, the Architect also has an important role to play for the Joker. Indeed, incomprehensible as it may be to the Joker, the Architect loves nothing more than putting a detailed plan in place - along with systems and processes - to ensure that not only does the money start rolling in, but that it keeps rolling in!

It's at this point that the second solution comes into play. With enough money to underwrite their day-to-day living expenses, the Joker does well to start investing in things **in which they're not personally involved**. Shares, property, pensions - all the stuff that doesn't light their fire **can** help them build wealth (especially using the power of compound interest over time) without them really having to lift a finger. Having the 'money work for them', rather than them 'having to work for the money' particularly appeals to the Joker. The first goal with outside investments is to create sufficient passive income to cover monthly living costs (both now and in the future) - and with that in place, the Joker gets to choose whether or not (or how much) they ever work again. Nothing could be more *incentivising* for the Joker than that whiff of freedom.

How to have difficult money conversations at home

Jokers prefer to 'live for today' and get bored easily. Their fear is that any discussion about money will be tedious at best - and at worst, may lead to yet another argument. Historically, and possibly from childhood, Jokers have come to associate financial conversations with some degree of unhappiness. Gently point out to a Joker that the goal is to build and use money to have more *fun* - and they'll suddenly start taking an interest. (Make sure to stick to 'no recriminations' though, as that's the only way to keep the Joker's *trust*. If there's been a problem in the past, acknowledge it, agree that 'We are where we are' and suggest working together to create a different outcome.) Finally, invite the Joker to take care of suggesting the venue for future conversations about money. Dinner out always appeals to the Joker.

When it comes to talking about money in business

The Joker is fairly happy talking about money in business - providing they've got enough in their wallet or bank account *now*. They tend to take the 'big picture' view and are at their happiest when talking about money and how it relates to fun things or exciting one-off projects. Trying to interest a Joker in discussions about monthly cashflow (or already-spent-expenses) isn't likely to generate anywhere near as much enthusiasm. In their shadow, Jokers are apt to spend money twice in their heads - once when they win the contract and the second time when their invoice is paid. Shadow Jokers find it easy to get into denial - and to change the subject - when money is tight.

The Joker's attitude to financial risk

However successful they are, Jokers live for the moment and tend to spend what they earn on having a good time - buying shiny things, enjoying dream holidays or socialising with their extended network. Often in denial about the need to plan for the future, it's only when big birthdays hit that they wonder how the party is going to continue as they age. Depression can kick in at this point. However, show them that investing can help them make money without much effort and they'll soon become enthusiasts. The

Jokers' need for thrills can make them more comfortable with risk than their financial capacity for loss may suggest is prudent.

How to persuade or sell to the Joker

The Joker likes to be connected - and armed with his or her 'little black book of contacts' - thrives on introducing new ideas to people. Showing the Joker how buying from you is going to expand their horizons is important - but helping them see how their life is going to be easier and more fun is vital, if they're going to part with their money.

Printed literature should be colourful and have emotional appeal - but frankly, they'd much prefer to watch a video (especially one that focuses on people.)

JOKERS AT WORK: As the boss

Joker bosses are fun to work with - on a good day. They inspire, encourage and persuade everyone to deliver just a tiny bit more than their previous personal best. When profits soar, everyone gets to celebrate. Great Joker bosses know to share the glory publicly but to take personal responsibility when things go wrong.

On a bad day however, things can be very different. And that's what makes working for a Joker boss both an adventure and an occasional nightmare. Who knows what mood the Joker boss will turn up in today? Will they suddenly give everyone the day off - or just as suddenly fire someone in a fit of pique?

It has to be said that Joker bosses aren't very predictable - and while that can keep things interesting for people on their team who thrive on variety and intrigue, it can be very unnerving for those who highly prize routine and security.

Individuals love nothing better than soaking up the sunshine that Joker bosses naturally emanate - but when they switch their attention elsewhere, they can inadvertently leave people in the 'shade' - breeding resentment.

While they're great communicators when it comes to selling, they're not always so good at ensuring that the people on their team actually know what's expected of them. Even if those people have job descriptions, a Joker has no compunction in switching them to a different role. Systems and processes are anathema to the Joker - but the smart ones see that they're vital if a business is to thrive. When they can afford it, they'll get someone else in to run that side of the business - it's just too boring to apply themselves to such a seemingly mundane activity on a regular basis.

Jokers can be mercurial - up one minute and down the next. To onlookers, Jokers seem to thrive on chaos. It is true, they do. Don't expect a Joker to have a tidy desk for long.

They also have a short attention span and can become thwarted by detail. One of the most powerful antidotes to their shambolic approach is for a Joker boss to hire a PA who can clean up behind them and coordinate things moving forward. Once they've proved that they have an eye for detail, can be trusted and have displayed their psychic abilities in terms of being able to interpret what the Joker *meant* - rather than what he or she *said* - then the PA has a secure role for life. They'll be revered and rewarded by the Joker (and as luck would have it, they'll have so much fun that they'll never want to leave).

As managers & colleagues

Jokers who work within an organisation are best suited to roles that revolve around people and not things. They're particularly unsuited to following systems and processes - and their low boredom threshold can lead to them playing the office clown.

Similarly, deadlines and pressure don't particularly motivate the Joker per se - but if they're interested in what they're doing and can see how their efforts will contribute to both the bigger picture and their own coffers, they'll actually get quite excited.

Younger Jokers require quite a lot of management in the early days and while they can be as much fun to have around as a young puppy, they also pose a threat to things getting done and shipped on time. Jokers like nothing more than distraction - so where possible, they should be given roles which offer plenty of variety.

Interestingly, Jokers are often good at managing other people. They're great communicators and they know how to inspire and motivate. They're also great delegators (well, if they can get someone else to do the work rather than do it themselves, then why not?). If they're put in charge of a sales team, they'll get great results - and they'll often incentivise their teams with what to outsiders look like ridiculous prizes, but which nonetheless do the job. (The Joker understands the importance of recognition - and leader boards, points and prizes all contribute to individuals on the team feeling *special*.)

Having said all that, the best Joker managers are often hard to manage. While they've taken great care to learn how to handle their team (who often become so loyal that they'd almost walk off the edge of a cliff to support their hero or heroine), they spectacularly fail to learn how to 'manage upwards'. This can lead to them getting into serious disputes with their up-line, which not only wastes everyone's time and energy but which can also seriously hamper the Joker manager's prospects for promotion.

But whatever their gifts and flaws, Jokers can be relied upon to make sure that the social cogs in the office wheel are regularly oiled - whether that's by organising fun events outside of hours or making sure that people's birthdays are celebrated. And as such, they contribute greatly to office morale.

JOKER: UNDERSTANDING THE SHADOW

In Jungian psychology, the 'shadow' refers to the 'unknown' or unconscious dark side of the personality which the ego does not recognise within itself (even if it's pretty obvious to everyone else!). It could even be said that until we identify and then 'own' our shadow aspect, it'll keep us trapped in self-sabotaging and self-defeating patterns. Just as unpalatably, the 'shadow' is the unowned part of us that manipulates others.

If it's any consolation, we all have a 'shadow'. For the Joker, the shadow plays out through their intense focus on living in the 'now' - neither learning the lessons from the past nor planning for the future. Having a good time is their number one goal - and they're prepared to be generous in order to have other people come and play with them.

Sadly though, they're not always able to differentiate between true friends and 'hangers-on' - and they can find themselves hurt and disappointed when people abandon them when the money runs out. And as Jokers often learn the hard way, those people you help and share with on the way 'up', aren't always there for you when the chips come tumbling down.

Their charismatic and fun nature can get the Joker into difficulty - it's not so much that they want to cause trouble, it's just that trouble somehow seems to find them. Their fun antics - often fuelled by alcohol - can escalate and more than a few Jokers have had the questionable joy of spending a night in the cells.

Those with looser morals still can find themselves spending longer behind bars for a variety of reasons - most probably: theft, brawling and fighting while under the influence of alcohol or drugs. Of course, with their propensity to make friends wherever they are, Jokers spending any length of time in prison often get to hone their criminal skills by learning from those more experienced than themselves, and thus a life of crime begins.

Generally unable to see the possible consequences of their behaviour from the outset, Jokers often find that the people who are in any way responsible for them (parents, teachers, employers) don't always entirely trust them. This makes the Joker cross - after all, they're perfectly capable of achieving excellence if they put their mind to it.

Jokers can be resentful of others' opinions of them. Sometimes they deal with this discomfort by 'playing to the gallery' while on other occasions, they simply scupper the outcome of an entire project - little realising that at the end of the day, they're simply sabotaging themselves.

To a greater or lesser degree - depending on their upbringing, Jokers are actually hiding their self-doubt and fear of not-being-good-enough under a facade of bravado. They keep the smiling face of their 'tragi-comedy' mask steadfastly glued in place - hoping to fool those around them into thinking that everything is OK. For some Jokers, this can lead to a life of superficiality but for others, even more dangerously, it can lead to deep seated feelings of isolation.

Jokers long to be recognised for all that they're capable of being. While they may not show it, they suffer deeply when others (who are often exhausted by the Joker's antics) put them down, rain on their parade or try to keep them small. Jokers thrive on freedom and long to express themselves - and rail against anyone or anything that threatens their physical, mental or emotional liberty.

Perhaps because of their own naturally uncomplicated and sunny nature, Jokers find it hard to believe that other people may have an agenda of their own (hidden or otherwise).

When Jokers are on the receiving end of others' negative comments and barbs, they fall into the trap of believing that it's because there's something wrong with **them** (the Joker). It simply never occurs to them that the people around them might be projecting their own lack of happiness - combined with their unacknowledged anger, fear or jealousy onto the seemingly happy-go-lucky Joker. Until they become aware of it, Jokers can find themselves unwittingly holding on to a lot of unprocessed and painful self-recrimination.

Bitter and resentful Jokers can end up feeling very sorry for themselves - and on a fast track to depression. Often they seek to drown their sorrows with alcohol - but while they may feel better in the short term, they fail to contemplate or learn from their situations, which can lead to history repeating itself again. And again.

Others can find themselves indulging in a series of meaningless relationships and one-night-stands, all in a bid to stave off loneliness. Smart Jokers eventually come to understand that one of their lessons in life is to learn to form a good relationship with **themselves** - something that they spend a lot of time trying to avoid by always making sure that they're in the company of others, having fun.

How the Joker can self-sabotage

The Joker often struggles to believe that a little more hard work in the present might yield much benefit in the future - which sadly means that their great potential isn't always fulfilled.

What the Joker deeply believes about themselves

Some deeply-held beliefs are positive while others emanate from the shadows. Intriguingly, these beliefs are often a variation on the same theme:

Light Belief: "While I love being the life and soul of the party, sometimes it feels like a bit of a responsibility too."

Shadow Belief: "I don't know when to 'stop'."

JOKER: HOW THEY APPROACH LIFE

In all relationships, the joyful, exuberant and fun-loving Joker has learned from the outset to expand their boundaries - and they love nothing more than exploring and experiencing everything that life has to offer.

They hate repetition and boredom and naturally gravitate to what's novel and exciting. They're life's early adopters - and while they can on occasion be lethargic when it comes to getting things done and dusted, their natural energy prevents them from being lazy - just so long as there is enough to keep their interest piqued.

Jokers know that their strong suit is living in the 'now' - and they gobble up every moment with almost breathless enthusiasm. Unless they're bored, in which case they can waste hours and hours on nothing in particular, with nothing to show for it in the end.

Things can go a bit pear-shaped for Jokers when it comes to planning for the future. Sure, they love being stimulated by the 'big picture' - particularly if it involves some fun and excitement - but if they're honest, they'd actually prefer someone else attends to the finer details.

Finally, Jokers - even by their own admission - can be a bit slap dash. Their sense of 'good enough' being 'good enough' can infuriate those around them who are more detail focused.

JOKER: AS A ROMANTIC PARTNER

Jokers are fun, they can be wonderfully romantic - and they're never boring! Talkative, inquisitive and on a permanent quest of discovery, life with a Joker can be a real joy. However, restrict their freedom, nag them and remind them constantly about their responsibilities in life and there's likely to be a sad ending. For Jokers, life can be a bit of a party - and their partners should expect to spend lots of time out socialising with family and friends. Holidays, trips out, weekends away - these bring a sense of adventure to the Joker, who loves nothing more than sharing with his or her beloved. Jokers tend not to enjoy spending lots of time on their own though, which can be difficult for some partners who need solitude to recharge their batteries.

Worth considering: Jokers in relationships hate the idea of being trapped and thrive in an atmosphere of freedom. Romantic by nature, they love 'being in love' and have big plans and dreams for the future. Some shun marriage as a 'tie', but those who choose to go down that path fair well *when* they (and their partner) believe that every day is a 'choice'. While Jokers can be fickle - or even unfaithful - when they find their *true soul mate*, they just 'know' and happily settle down for life. Encourage, inspire and reward a Joker and they'll achieve great things for the partnership.

How the Joker handles money in a relationship

If they're in the right job role, Jokers can be great providers - but they're not the best at running the family finances on a day-to-day basis because (as they'll freely admit) money can all too easily slip through their fingers. Unlikely to hold onto their receipts, Jokers tend to dislike even the mere idea of budgeting.

Jokers without access to money feel stifled - and a stifled Joker isn't fun to be around. Indeed, when a Joker feels that his or her liberty is curtailed, they're likely to act out (either by becoming argumentative, sulky or by simply walking out - either for good, or at least until they see the error of their ways).

The Joker's desire to have everything 'now' make them good targets for banks and credit companies - and it's not unusual for Jokers to rack up considerable debt (with or without their partner's knowledge).

It also has to be said that Jokers aren't averse to telling little white lies about just how much they've spent. Jokers tend not to think about their future - so their spouse may need to do the job for the both of them.

JOKER: AS A PARENT

Jokers see parenting as an adventure. Having retained child-like wonder themselves, they're capable of making their offspring's childhoods magical and memorable for all the right reasons. Jokers inflict as few rules as possible on their children, who are often allowed to stay up late, try alcohol at a young age and watch what some would perceive as 'unsuitable' television programmes. Other children often look on with envy. Joker parents believe that there's more to life than school - and don't overly scold for poor grades. Quite often, when a Joker's child grows up, they secretly wish that their parents had actually encouraged and pushed them to achieve more. Joker parents buy cool things for their kids, unconsciously recognising that their child's self-confidence grows when they're accepted by their peers. Joker parents understand all about self-confidence being the key to success in later life, and they'll do all they can to foster it in their children.

Worth considering: Unhappy Jokers don't make great parents. They're not only capable of neglecting their children's needs but can create a role-reversal in their offspring, who sadly discover that the only way to survive is by becoming an overly responsible mini-adult.

JOKER: AS A CHILD

Joker children are a delight. They love learning and their curiosity and wonder about the world are captivating. Their sunny nature makes the Joker child easy to manage and entertain - although their boundless energy can leave their parents worn out at the end of the day. Joker children tend to see school as one big social opportunity for play. Being forced to learn by rote bores them rigid - but inspire their imaginations and they can develop a life long interest in a particular subject.

Often living in their own fantasy world, Joker children love films, video games and music - particularly if it's fast pace and exciting. While they love money (what child doesn't?), they're disinclined to save it, instead spending it on whatever shiny thing takes their fancy in the moment. If, however, they have their eye on a bigger prize (like an expensive guitar or a bicycle for example) they can amass the money they need at astonishing speed.

It's less that they save it, more that they're able to charm the adults around them to part with their hard-earned cash just for the fun of it. Or if that fails, they'll persuade those very same adults to overpay them to do some household chores. This is of course, how they learn their superlative sales skills, which will stand them in good stead as adults.

Worth considering: Joker children can develop great reserves of charm - and they're often able to use it to cover up their lack of desire for hard work. It's worth checking a Joker child's work before handing them the cash, as closer inspection often reveals that the task has been done shoddily, if at all.

JOKER: HOW THEY RELATE TO TIME

Jokers often run out of time because they're just not life's planners. They live in the moment and can get deeply engrossed in whatever it is that's captured their imagination. Punctuality really isn't their thing - and they dismiss those who are sticklers for it as 'stuffy'. Optimists that they are, Jokers tend not to build in sufficient contingency time for anything. They're able to tell more than one funny story about how they missed an important flight - seemingly not having learned the lesson from the first experience.

How the Joker breaches boundaries around time

The Joker can waste time by putting off those tasks that seem tedious today - only to find that they're bigger (with more serious implications) tomorrow.

JOKER: WHAT THEY WEAR

Jokers love clothes and enjoy looking good. While they like to be appropriately dressed for the occasion, they'll make sure that they stand out, even if only a little. Jokers enjoy the fact that they're memorable - and they know that the right clothes can really help them in this endeavour. They usually love shopping and often have bulging wardrobes full of bright and fashionable clothes. They're less likely to buy 'classic pieces' that'll stand the test of time, preferring to ring the changes each season. They love popular designer items and when they find something that they just can't do without, they're not averse to buying the same thing in every colour and putting it all on their credit card without a second thought.

HOW OTHER - HIGH SCORING - 'MONEY TYPES' CAN INFLUENCE THE JOKER

Joker - Pharaoh:

A natural leader, this individual also makes a fabulous host, promoter and ambassador. People enjoy being around them because they make business *fun*, but there's absolutely no doubt who's the boss. They recognise that success in business is all about relationships - both with their team and out in the marketplace.

Watch out for: This individual needs to understand that the people they're in business with just love it when they're the centre of the Joker-Pharaoh's attention - but can feel rejected and resentful when that attention is directed elsewhere.

Moving forwards: The Joker-Pharaoh needs to recognise the importance of acknowledging others and allowing them to shine.

Joker - Magician:

This individual inspires others to achieve what can look like the impossible!

The entrepreneurial Magician is great at spotting opportunities and with the Joker's natural relationship building skills, this individual is able to tap into their extensive list of contacts to ensure that their exciting vision gets turned into reality.

Watch out for: The Joker-Magician needs to learn that the excitement of sharing ideas with anyone and everyone who'll listen can sometimes get in the way of actually **actioning** them! Talk by itself is cheap, so they need to make plans - and stick to them - for turning their ideas into reality.

Moving forwards: The Joker-Magician needs to adopt the 'power of the deadline' to motivate themselves and others.

Joker - Angel:

This individual combines their relationship-building qualities with their desire to make things better for everyone. They're one of the rare people who can see the problems facing the world - and are able to pull an army together to do something about it. They inspire where others may fear to tread.

Watch out for: In their frenzy to make the world a better place, the Joker-Angel can sometimes forget about the needs of those closer to home, including themselves.

Moving forwards: The Joker-Angel need to learn to prioritise themselves and their loved ones - physically and emotionally.

Joker - Architect:

This individual's BIG plans for their community come to fruition - and they achieve this by creating a tight framework and measurable action plan for others to follow. They have a very pragmatic and logical approach and know that projects are only manifested through **people**. Little phases them and whatever they set out to achieve, they achieve with flying colours.

Watch out for: The Joker-Architect can enjoy tinkering with the details to such an extent that they miss the big picture altogether. Instead, they should inspire others with the big picture and share the details only as necessary.

Moving forwards: The Joker-Architect needs to understand that successful leaders share the credit but take the blame.

Joker - Prisoner:

This individual is able to see what *isn't* working and what most definitely needs to be fixed. Fuelled by a heady mixture of injustice and determination to put 'wrongs' right, they're easily able to attract people to fight alongside them for those causes in which they passionately believe.

Watch out for: The Joker-Prisoner can end up fighting for the sake of it! These individuals need to leave their egos behind and follow the wisdom of their hearts to ensure that what they're seeking to change is in everyone's best interests, not just their own.

Moving forwards: The Joker-Prisoner needs to learn to keep others on side by inspiring them with a positive vision - and they also do well to remember that people are more inclined to want to fight *for* - rather than *against* - something.

THE ANGEL

ANGELS love taking care of everyone else – indeed, they're happy only when everyone else around them is happy. They're great at understanding people and making relationships – and their empathic skills mean that people often confide their deepest secrets to the Angel.

What can help the ANGEL: With their valuable relationship skills, Angels make sure that everyone gets what they need, when they need it – no wonder they're so popular. However, they need to make sure that they've included themselves in the equation as well, by valuing their own time and resources. Just as importantly, Angels need to have a clear idea of what they want out of life too.

The trap that could undermine the ANGEL: Feeling 'needed' makes the Angel feel good - however, their behaviours can easily tip into 'people pleasing'. In order to avoid others taking advantage of them, Angels need to learn to put themselves first. It may by now be an old cliche, but the advice to 'Fix your own oxygen mask first before helping anyone else' has to have been invented with the Angel in mind.

Three Insight Questions for Angels:

1. Am I clear in what I want to achieve and am I communicating this clearly to others?

2. Am I focusing my attention and activity in a directed way, or am I scattering my energy in too many directions?

3. Am I putting my family, my colleagues and my friends 'first' to such an extent that I'm not getting to live the life I want?

ANGEL GLOBAL ROLE: PEACEMAKER

Angels are kind hearted, generous and loving people. They see the best in everyone - and quickly build up a reputation for being forgiving, loving and compassionate.

They love helping others and have a deep seated belief that the world should be the way they know in their hearts that it **could** be. They often feel that they're being 'called' - and are responsible for - creating their vision of 'heaven on earth', which they carry as a blueprint deep within their psyche.

Angels are compassionate souls - the ones who want to create peace in the world and who are determined to help all those who are less well off than themselves. (And there are a lot of people who Angels believe need help, so they often have a somewhat uneasy feeling that their work is 'never done'.)

Idealists, peacemakers and nurturers, Angels love being at the heart of things - and enjoy nothing more than a sense of being needed. When they're not trying to heal the world, they focus their attentions closer to home, doing all they can to make life easier for everyone around them (and once again, they find themselves feeling that however much they do, they should be doing more. Much more.).

Their empathic nature, coupled with their uncanny intuitive abilities, ensure that Angels are the first port of call for people who are in any kind of trouble - whether they want a shoulder to cry on or need to borrow some money.

Angels hate conflict - and would rather not stand their ground, even if it means losing out personally - rather than risk falling out with someone. This results in some people believing that Angels are weak or a pushover - but while Angels will put up and shut up when it comes to themselves, they'll courageously stand and fight to the bitter end when it comes to defending other people.

Great advocates and staunch allies for everyone around them - they often find themselves bewildered when people bicker, squabble and fight. Their natural reaction is to use their highly developed empathic skills to first try to understand the situation - and then do all they can to mediate and make things better.

In order to thrive, Angels first need to decide what is important to them - and then learn how to protect and defend their own boundaries.

KEY ROLES: Peacemaker, Counsellor, Empath

KEY BELIEF: "When everyone else is happy, I can then be happy"

KEY LESSON: Making sure that they take care of themselves

KEY STRENGTH: Intuition

KEY DESIRE: Harmony

ANGEL PERSONAL DRIVE: GIVING

While big-hearted Angels put everyone else at the centre of their own Universe, when it comes to looking after themselves, it's a completely different matter. Rarely do Angels pause and think about what they need. Rarer still is the Angel who stops to consider what they want!

Indeed, because their focus is so much on other people, Angels can ignore their own needs to an extent that just wouldn't be fathomable to anyone else. They can even forget to eat or fail to give themselves enough rest and relaxation time, which can lead to burnout. With their highly developed sense of duty and obligation, Angels can find themselves hurt and disappointed when the people around them don't reciprocate with the same levels of care and good deeds.

As care givers, Angels are notoriously bad at asking for help for themselves - even (and perhaps, especially) when they really need it. They believe that they should always be able to do more - and their self value comes from being able to stand back and see how much they've done for everyone else.

When Angels accept the invitation to love themselves as much as they care for others, their lives transform and become joyful, harmonious and abundant.

Looking back over their childhoods, it usually becomes apparent that Angels didn't have the easiest time of it. Often they were put into positions of responsibility at an age that simply wasn't appropriate - which leads to them becoming overly responsible for everyone else when they mature into adulthood.

Sadly, for some Angels - especially those born into families where violence and victimisation were the norm, their only way to survive as children was to learn how to keep the people around them happy, which if left unchecked, can lead to a life of people-pleasing.

Partly because of their backgrounds and partly because of their natural inclinations, Angels are fascinated by psychology and personal development work. While they may start out wanting to develop their innate skills in order to help others, the magic really happens when they learn to apply what they learn to **themselves**. Indeed, choosing to put themselves at the heart of their own lives is the greatest gift they can give themselves.

ANGEL: RELATIONSHIP WITH MONEY

Angels have an interesting relationship with money - seeing it mostly as a tool with which to help others. The more they have, the more they believe they can do to make other people's lives easier - whether it's loved ones, impoverished people in far off lands or distressed animals.

While this is an admirable trait, when taken to the extreme it can cause problems for Angels (and even their families, who can find themselves called upon to bail out a yet-again-financially-distressed Angel.)

Indeed, some Angels who are actually short of money, have been known to borrow money on their credit cards to help out others - with no expectation of getting the money back. The fact that they'll end up paying interest on the loan for months, if not years to come, doesn't enter their heads.

It is also not unusual for Angels to use their very-hard-earned salaries to prop up less hard-working partners, family members and even friends. With their dislike of confrontation, Angels tend to avoid asking for any loans to be repaid, preferring instead to trust that those around them will 'do the right thing'. They rarely do.

What Angels have to learn is that there are people who are unlike them in the world - people whose focus is pure self-interest. An Angel would only ever ask someone for financial assistance if they had absolutely no other option (and even then, they'd be likely to explain the requirement for a loan in terms of someone else, like a child, needing help).

Wanting to believe that others share their similar 'giving' outlook on the world, Angels can come horribly unstuck when others fail to behave honourably. While it wouldn't occur to an Angel not to repay a loan - even if they end up almost beggaring themselves in the process - there are plenty of unscrupulous people out in the world who simply see an Angel as a rather accommodating cash cow. And when that particular Angel's funds have been exhausted, the 'takers' simply move on to their next 'innocent victim', leaving a confused, hurt and impoverished Angel in their wake.

While everyone around them might have seen it 'coming', the Angel doesn't. After all, Angels have high ideals and often believe that they are the cause of other people's poor behaviours - and so berate themselves for not earning more, or sharing more, which would (in their minds) have preserved the relationship.

Angels are life's carers - and givers - and often believe that they're not clever enough to earn mega bucks or run a business. Maths was never their strong subject - and they've come to associate maths and money together. Female Angels are often patronised by their menfolk (usually starting with their fathers) who encourage them to believe that 'money' is men's work.

This results in Angels tending to give their power - especially their financial power - away to 'cleverer' men, who they believe are simply better at knowing how to handle money. Unfortunate Angels sometimes discover that the partners they'd completely trusted have made rash decisions - and that the roof over their family's heads has been put in jeopardy. Even in those circumstances, rather than blaming their partner, the Angel blames themselves for not knowing better. After all, Angels have perfected the art of self-recrimination.

Taking care of ourselves - looking after our own needs, wants and desires - is actually the most selfless gift we can give others.

As in the other areas of their lives, Angels need to learn to set boundaries, to politely say 'no' (rather than 'yes') as an immediate response to a request for financial assistance - and to recognise that **the one person for whom they must take responsibility is themselves.** Many will rail against such advice. Those who take it - and who decide to learn about money - will find that actually, they're rather good at it. Erring on the side of caution, they won't do anything rash with money when it comes to investments - not least, because they'll be all too aware of how others could be affected negatively.

Until they learn to value themselves - and to see what value they bring to others - Angels can often end up earning less than their peers, purely because they've not wanted to risk the confrontation of asking for a raise or promotion. Indeed, at a job interview, an Angel is most likely to accept - with gratitude - whatever salary they're offered, rather than negotiate.

Equally, Angels can fall into the trap of doing longer hours and more unpaid overtime than their colleagues. Of course, their managers love them - and Angels can delight in their feathers being stroked in gratitude. But what they may be less aware of though, is that their line managers will be loathe to promote them - after all, how could one afford to lose someone who'll uncomplainingly work hard, and who doesn't demand overtime pay?

Ideal careers for Angels

Hospitality | Medicine | Customer Service | Teaching

People Management | Human Resources

Counselling | Therapy | Beauty

Angels who watch their lazier colleagues get promoted over their heads can become despondent, wondering why they aren't good enough - and what it is that they need to do better. They'd do well to recognise that 99 times out of 100, they're great at what they do - and simply need to work on their own self-esteem and self-perception.

When an Angel starts to really see what others see in them, their self doubt simply melts away. Giving generously to others - even when they can't afford it either financially or in terms of time - is the hallmark of the Angel. After all, they adore being needed. For some, it gives them a sense of fulfilment and purpose while for others, it's more about justifying their existence. Either way, it doesn't take a lot for an Angel to be pushed into approval-seeking or people-pleasing behaviours.

Angels often fear that they're not great with money - but actually, that's not really true. The real reason that they don't always have a healthy bank balance is because they're always focusing on how they can help other people (often at a big cost to themselves).

And because they're very in tune with their intuitive and empathic side, some people can mistake this for weakness. Of course, nothing would be further from the truth - it takes real strength to be open and when the Angel genuinely wants to help others, they've already at least partially overcome the selfish demands of the ego.

However, ruthless people can take advantage of the Angel's good nature - believing that they'll drop everything to help - even if it means dipping into their life savings - if they're given a good heart-tugging sob story. And make no mistake, when those ruthless people have taken just about everything the Angel's ever had, they won't be grateful and hang around - they'll be off to find their next 'host', money-suckers that they are! (And unless the Angel has already done a fair amount of work on themselves, they'll probably feel inexplicably guilty that they couldn't have done more.)

To counteract this dangerous tendency, Angels can find it helpful to start looking out for themselves as though they were their own 'best friend'. Angels tend to fall into the trap of giving and giving - so it's worth asking them what they'd say to a friend who was exhibiting the same behaviours. The Angel would, of course, naturally remind them to take care of themselves too.

Angels need to learn to value themselves...

They also need to watch out for unscrupulous employers who sometimes craft wonderfully creative, 'valid' reasons for why they can't pay the Angel what they're worth. These same employers will have also perfected the art of telling the Angel just how much they'd be **valued** on the team. Positive strokes can, unfortunately, be the Angel's undoing. While their 'need to be needed' may well be rewarded - the Angel will sadly have lost out on what they could have been earning - and saving. Save from an early age and you'll have time on your side, through the magic of compound interest.

In order to make money, the first step is for the Angel to recognise the **value** that they bring to others. If the Angel can't see it for themselves, then they should - without ego - ask others to help them identify their specific gifts and talents.

The second step is for the Angel to recognise that they may have fallen foul of the many lies people spread about the 'evils' of having money. Agreed, the relentless pursuit of money for its own sake isn't helpful. But when the Angel begins to see that the more money they have, the more **they can do** to make the world a better place for both themselves and others, the quicker they begin to change their perspective.

The Angel needs to learn how to feel comfortable with the idea of living in abundance - so that they can fully live out their purpose in life. (Special hint for Angels: You're not here to suffer.)

Making the magic happen...

The next steps are for the Angel to learn to budget effectively, to request employers or clients pay them what they're worth, to protect their boundaries and to choose to save, even if it's only tiny amounts at the start. (Often, when we don't have enough money, we 'give up' mentally and buy something to 'cheer ourselves up'. We may feel a bit better for a short while, but the money we spent has gone for ever. When we start saving or investing what we would have idly spent, magic seems to happen - with money starting to come in from unexpected sources.)

When Angels drop their fear of money (and especially when they realise that they're meant to have money), they rapidly learn how to create a good *relationship* with it - nurturing it with the care and attention they historically used to give away to everyone else.

How to have difficult money conversations at home

Angels often avoid the subject of Money as they know it can make other people feel very uncomfortable - and they tend to feel good themselves only when everyone else around them is happy. But ask an Angel for their input in planning what's best for everyone - and it's a different story. Remember that Angels tend to put everyone else first and leave themselves out of the equation, so make sure to keep checking in that their needs are being met too. They'll thank you for it - even if only inwardly - and this way, the Angel will avoid explosive resentment building up for later. Finally, acknowledge everything that an Angel does - often they unwittingly feel 'lesser than' and powerless because their contribution to life can't always be measured in financial terms.

When it comes to talking about money in business

The Angel is often uncomfortable talking about money in business - partly because they're afraid the topic will make others uncomfortable and partly because they don't like asking for things for themselves. In their power, Angels know that when they're paid well for a 'good job', they're able to take better care of themselves and their loved ones. In their shadow, Angels can allow the people around them to 'dictate terms' and then quietly seethe with resentment a short while later. Afraid that being assertive will be mistaken for being aggressive or demanding, Shadow Angels prefer to dance around the topic of money for as long as possible - especially when the discussion is with people they know well.

The Angel's attitude to financial risk

Priding themselves on caring for others, Angels like to keep the peace, even if this means not standing up for what's in their best interests financially. They've often struggled for money in the past, having given a lot of it away to help those they care about. As they get older, they can get resentful when they begin to see that it's *never* going to be 'their turn'. The smart ones subsequently learn that they must look after themselves first, in order to be able to help others. Angels have a tendency to defer to those they believe to be 'cleverer' (particularly to men) - with the result that when things go wrong financially, they often play the 'victim card'.

How to persuade or sell to the Angel

The Angel likes to feel 'valued' - and to feel that any kind of deal is collaborative rather than merely transactional. Relationships have the highest priority for Angels and they want to know that any kind of purchase helps others out too. Indeed, nothing makes them happier than being able to see how a specific purchase they're making can contribute (through an organisation's social responsibility scheme for example) to a wider - possibly global - community. Printed literature needs to show 'faces' and happy 'people' (or animals!).

ANGELS AT WORK: as the boss

Angel bosses always make it easy for everyone else - and often quietly pick up the slack when other people don't perform. Too much of this, and the Angel boss gets burned out.

They are acutely aware of how other people feel - which is why they tread carefully when managing others. Unfortunately, they tread so carefully that others don't always have a clear understanding of exactly what's expected of them. While most people achieve their best results through a mixture of 'carrot and stick', Angels are deeply uncomfortable at the prospect of wielding the said stick - which means that work-shy employees are all too able to take advantage of their good nature.

In owner-managed businesses, Angels can be inclined to prop up the organisation with their own funds (or even by re-mortgaging their home) rather than take any harsh business decisions, like 'letting people go'. Often Angels will only make cuts when all other financing avenues have been exhausted, which can leave them in debt. They can then get resentful when the people they've tried to support (perhaps by taking a reduced salary themselves) simply leave or move to other positions without a backward glance. Wise Angels recognise the experience as another lesson in the need to create boundaries and the invitation to put themselves at the centre of their lives.

Angel bosses always do their absolut best to be understanding - and to treat everyone fairly. They can be overly generous in this approach - and surprised to find that their kindness with one team member can lead to reciprocal resentment in another. "Why can't they play nicely and just see that I'm trying to do the best for everyone?" is their lament.

Business owning Angels are often great at understanding their market place - and recognise that *sales is about relationships* and not simply closing the deal. Their organisations offer great service and happy clients and customers often give them glowing testimonials and recommendations. In order to ensure that their businesses reach their maximum potential, Angel bosses need to be *clear* with all those around them. As well as setting expectations - including targets and goals - and providing comfortable and nourishing workplace facilities, Angel bosses also need to clearly set out the consequences of what will happen to staff who underperform.

As managers & colleagues

Once again, Angels who are working for someone else need to be aware of their own boundaries - as their tendency will be to take up the slack for their colleagues (or people working under them) as they hate to see someone getting into trouble.

Keen to help - and loving being appreciated, Angels will often step in to help someone else who is struggling - while at the same time, leaving their own work unfinished. This can lead to run-ins with line managers who accuse the Angel of slacking - which infuriates and bewilders the Angel who had confidently been expecting praise for 'saving the day'.

Angels need to learn that - as with money - they should only step in to help others if and when their **own needs and duties have been fulfilled**. Often it needs to be spelled out to them that they will solely be judged for the results they achieve (or don't achieve) in their *own* job - and that 'helping others' is not an acceptable excuse for an uncompleted task.

Angels can be inclined to stay late to keep their boss happy - who in all likelihood, will be very happy indeed to see the Angel working unpaid overtime (in return for the very occasional 'thank you' or bunch of flowers.) Conversely, an Angel - irrespective of their position at work - who has someone sick at home, will expect everyone to completely understand if they need to take time off (however suddenly) and certainly don't expect to be questioned on the matter.

Having said all of that, Angels tend to be very popular in the workplace as they're always prepared to provide a listening ear and advice - often very good advice.

Finally, Angels are also the ones who make sure that people's birthdays are remembered - and will probably be the ones organising both the cake and the whip-round for a gift too.

ANGEL: UNDERSTANDING THE SHADOW

In Jungian psychology, the 'shadow' refers to the 'unknown' or unconscious dark side of the personality which the ego does not recognise within itself (even if it's pretty obvious to everyone else!). It could even be said that until we identify and then 'own' our shadow aspect, it'll keep us trapped in self-sabotaging and self-defeating patterns. Just as unpalatably, the 'shadow' is the unowned part of us that manipulates others.

If it's any consolation, we all have a 'shadow'. For the Angel, the shadow plays out through the need for approval and acceptance from others. What can seem like generosity to the Angel can, on occasion, be a form of manipulation. After all, who's going to dare confront a generous, kind Angel?

We've all met people who seek to 'buy' us - and while it can seem flattering at first, it can all very quickly become too much. An Angel may feel that they're being kind - but the recipient can quickly sense that they're somehow indebted, which often leaves them feeling so uncomfortable that they begin to give the Angel a wide berth. This hurts the Angel, who tries even harder to give - in order to get the approval they so crave.

And thus the pattern is set to repeat.

Shadow Angels have a tremendous appetite for recognition and appreciation - and unless they're very aware of their motives, they're very skilled at gently twisting their good deeds into powerful guilt-inducing tools. Unfortunately for Angels, guilt is often the precursor to resentment - which can create an unexpected backlash.

Angels are prone to co-dependent relationships, in which each partner has a 'need' that at least initially, is supplied by the relationship itself. For example, 'givers' and 'takers' are often drawn together. The 'giver' can appear to be sweetness and light on the surface - and receive many plaudits for their efforts - but actually, unless they're very self-aware, they can be the ones with a hidden agenda. How? Their self-esteem and identity come from being perceived as a 'good person' - which means that they always need people to 'help' in order to preserve their self-image of being 'good'. It's in their darker interests then, not to have the people they're trying to help become self-sufficient or 'better', because then the Angel would be in danger of no longer being 'needed'. This state of affairs can keep people locked in an unhealthy relationship - sometimes for years.

Angels are prone to being manipulated and are the most likely of all the 'Money Types' to fall prey to people who have narcissistic tendencies. The Narcissist lures **them** in by being hyper-appreciative of the Angel's delightful qualities and once they have them hooked, they start playing power games and treating the Angel badly. Bewildered, the Angel resorts to doing what they do best - trying to please. The painful cycle repeats. Rather than seeing the bad behaviour in the other, the Angel - very possibly in a throwback to their own childhood - believes that there must be something wrong with **them**. This belief is deep rooted and until it is recognised and removed, the Angel is often doomed to painful relationships across the spectrum of romance, family and friendships. All of this hurt in their personal lives can leave the Angel feeling bemused and as they grow older, they become life's victims or martyrs - or both. The only antidote is self-awareness, which is most easily achieved through a programme of personal development and in some cases, therapy.

Used to being able to rely on themselves and having others rely on them, Angels quickly learn to take responsibility - even from a very young age. Unsurprisingly, Angels can easily slip into taking **over-responsibility** for others - leading to negative consequences. As well as the Angel feeling burdened and ultimately resentful, the other person also becomes angry as they can feel both 'controlled' and not 'trusted'.

Once Angels understand that life is about **choices -** and that they can do something (or not) out of choice rather than obligation, something deep begins to shift within them and they start operating from a higher vibration - leaving them happier and more empowered.

How the Angel can self-sabotage

Angels often have a seeming **inability** to recognise that their motive for putting others first isn't always altruistic and can sometimes be manipulative. This can lead to unhealthy co-dependent relationships.

What the Angel deeply believes about themselves

Some deeply-held beliefs are positive while others emanate from the shadows. Intriguingly, these beliefs are often a variation on the same theme:

Light Belief: "Helping everyone else brings me so much joy that I just want to do more and more!"

Shadow Belief: "I'm not good enough."

ANGEL: HOW THEY APPROACH LIFE

In all relationships, the naturally giving, kind and loving Angel needs to learn to protect themselves and their boundaries - choosing what they want and leading their own lives, rather than being a 'bit part' in other people's. The word they need to learn most is 'no'!

Angels fare much better when they create a strategy for themselves that allows them to press the 'pause button' before accepting unwanted invitations (rather than risk causing offence) or rushing to help others (irrespective of whether or not they have the personal resources to do so).

It can help to try answering all invitations with, "Let me have a think about that and I'll get back to you". This buys the Angel some reflection time and avoids them getting into something that they didn't want to do (or having to back out later and finding themselves rapidly earning a reputation for being 'flaky').

ANGEL: AS A ROMANTIC PARTNER

People love having a romantic relationship with the Angel because they're so caring - and always put others before themselves. Angels are gentle, loving, kind - and keen to make sure that their soul mates have everything they could possibly wish for (and more besides!). They're also good at making home life a wonderful haven - from creating a beautiful, comfortable sanctuary with fabulous interior design or cooking delicious and nourishing meals from scratch. Angels are also appreciated for their thoughtfulness when it comes to celebrating birthdays and anniversaries - and their generosity with gifts knows no bounds.

Worth considering: Their giving nature and tendency to put others' needs before their own can lead to some people taking advantage of Angels. They should learn to listen to their intuition when it comes to their partner and to make their own needs and desires equally important. Angels should recognise that they need to 'step up' when it comes to *money* in the relationship - as they have a tendency to give their power away. (As they get older, Angels can become bitter and angry - leading to passive aggressiveness - when they come to see that they've 'given' so much to a seemingly ungrateful partner and have received very little back in return.) They would also do well to understand too, that by being so wonderful to their partners, Angels can create feelings of inadequacy in them as they come to realise that they will never be able to live up to the high standards that have been set. Finally, Angels already know that a lot of pleasure comes from 'giving' - and they should learn that sometimes, it's really kind to allow their *partner* the pleasure of giving.

How Angels handle money in a relationship

Priding themselves on caring for others, Angels like to keep the peace, even if this means not standing up for what's in their own best interests financially. They have often struggled for money in the past, having given a lot of it away to help those they care about - whose needs they perceived as being even greater than their own. Again, as they get older, they can get resentful when they begin to see that it's never going to be 'their turn'. Smart Angels subsequently learn that they have to look after themselves first, in order to be able to help others.

ANGEL: AS A PARENT

Parents often have a strong Angel quality, and perhaps unsurprisingly, this is particularly prevalent in mothers, for whom putting their children first comes naturally. Children of Angel parents will feel nourished, blessed and loved unconditionally and will often grow up blissfully unaware of the many sacrifices their parents made on their behalf. Angel parents are also popular with their children's friends - offering understanding, caring and well thought out advice (together with lots of tempting snacks and treats!). Angel parents delight in creating the kind of childhood they themselves would have enjoyed (but often didn't) and hope that their efforts will give their own offspring lifelong happy memories.

Worth considering: In their attempt to make life as easy as they can for their offspring, Angels should make sure that they don't inadvertently take their power away. Children need to grow up feeling that they're trusted to make good decisions for themselves. Angel parents can unintentionally 'smother' their children - leaving them feeling embarrassed at best and controlled or 'entitled' at worst. Parents are role models for their children and if Angel parents give everything away without making sure that their own needs are taken care of first, then their children will grow up to do the same. Children of Angels also need to learn that there is a considerable difference between giving out of love...and sacrificing oneself out of a sense of 'obligation'.

ANGEL: AS A CHILD

While some children can be thoughtless and self-focused, this is not so with the Angel child, who loves nothing more than pleasing everyone around them (particularly the adults). Gentle by nature, they abhor conflict, whether it's their parents arguing, siblings teasing them or bullying at school. Their kind and compassionate hearts can see them doing things for charity at a young age (whether that's raising money through a sponsored activity or giving their time to volunteer for a cause that's close to their heart).

Worth considering: The most empathic and sensitive of the 'Money Types' children, the Angel child can be prone to unwittingly absorbing the thoughts, feelings and emotions of all those around them, without realising that they're doing so. Indeed, they're often not able to tell whether it's 'their stuff' or other people's, which can lead to them feeling bad and inclined to take on too much responsibility, too young. They become very adept at walking on egg shells around difficult, angry or depressed people and need to learn to stand their ground, ask for what they want and be 'complete' within themselves.

ANGEL: HOW THEY RELATE TO TIME

For Angels, there is never enough time. With the demands of other people uppermost in their mind, Angels need to be gently reminded that taking time out for themselves is a good thing. They may be persuaded by the thought that if they don't take at least some 'me time', then they'll get ill - and if they're ill, someone else will have to look after them (a thought that makes them very uncomfortable indeed). While Angels hate the idea of keeping others waiting, they often actually find themselves arriving late for appointments - either because they were helping someone else on the way or because they were thinking about what else they needed to get done. Angels are great at multi-tasking, after all, they believe that the more you can get ticked off a to-do list, the more time there is to get even more done.

How the Angel breaches boundaries around time

Angels can waste time by putting everyone else's needs first and not attending to their own - which means that things have to reach catastrophic (and often expensive) proportions before being given the required attention.

Often this results in some unplanned but enforced time-off. The danger is that when the Angel starts to feel any better at all, they start doing all they can to make up for lost time when it comes to catching up with chores and helping other people - with the result that they find themselves fast-tracked on to burn-out all over again.

ANGEL: WHAT THEY WEAR

Angels tend to be practical and like to dress comfortably - often with looser layers. After all, with all those people to help they don't want to be constricted in any way. They often choose colourful garments and when they get invited anywhere, they make sure that they at least look 'clean and decent' in honour of their hosts. Shoes and boots need to be comfortable - but preferably stylish. Angels aren't frumps - but they're not big spenders on clothes and accessories believing that there's a lot more good that they could be doing with their cash.

HOW OTHER - HIGH SCORING - 'MONEY TYPES' CAN INFLUENCE THE ANGEL

Angel - Pharaoh:

This individual leads where others may fear to tread. The Angel-Pharaoh is able to combine their desire to make things better for everyone with their inherent leadership qualities. They're one of the rare people who can see the problems facing the world - and have the courage to do something about it.

Watch out for: Determined to make the world a better place, the Angel-Pharaoh can sometimes forget about the needs of those closer to home, including themselves.

Moving forwards: The Angel-Pharaoh needs to learn to prioritise themselves and their loved ones - physically and emotionally.

Angel - Magician:

This individual is able to bring entrepreneurial vision to the projects with which they're involved. This means that they can see what needs to happen and how to turn it into reality. They also inherently know how to 'tick the right boxes' for other stakeholders too, so that they'll want to play ball as well. They use their empathic, kind and diplomatic skills to bring projects to fruition.

Watch out for: While they're good at ensuring that deals work for everyone, the Angel-Magician needs to remember that 'everyone' *includes* them too.

Moving forwards: The Angel-Magician needs to learn to avoid making deals on the hoof, and to consider things from all angles.

Angel - Joker:

With their legendary ability to help people feel better about themselves, this individual is able to encourage and energise others. They inspire, challenge and coach people to be the very best they can be. People love being around the Angel-Joker as they always feel better after being in their company. The Angel-Joker sees the best in everyone, forgives easily and enjoys 'spreading the love'. They're also great at highlighting just how much we all have to be grateful for - and whenever they're around, there's often an atmosphere of celebration.

Watch out for: With so much focus on other people, the Angel-Joker can sometimes forget about the needs of those closer to home, including themselves. This can leave them drained and on the road to burnout.

Moving forwards: The Angel-Joker needs to learn to take time out regularly to re-energise themselves - physically and emotionally.

Angel - Architect:

With the ability to put their BIG world-enhancing plans into place, this individual achieves success by creating an easily-understood framework and measurable action plan for others to follow. They have a very pragmatic and logical approach. Nothing phases them and whatever they set out to achieve, they achieve with flying colours.

Watch out for: The Angel-Architect can come across as somewhat serious, deep or intense, which might be off-putting for some people who are more comfortable with the lighter, more entertaining and superficial side of life. They need to remember that when people are intimidated - for whatever reason - they don't perform at their best.

Moving forwards: The Angel-Architect should keep inspiring people by shining the light on how the work they're doing is contributing to the *bigger picture*.

Angel - Prisoner:

This individual is able to see what ISN'T working and what most definitely needs to be fixed. Fuelled by a heady mixture of injustice and determination to put 'wrongs' right, they're driven to fight to the end for those causes in which they passionately believe. They're better at fighting for others than for themselves. Often they ignore their own needs, and later complain that life isn't fair. On occasion, they can tip over into playing the 'martyr'.

Watch out for: Prisoners can be 'created' because Angels - too focused on everyone around them - keep giving all their resources away to others. All too often, it's more comfortable for Angels to focus on helping others, leaving themselves out. Sooner or later, this leads to resentment and fatigue. Used wisely, the Prisoner aspect can help shine a light on what's not working for the Angel - inviting this individual to explore *inwards*, rather than repeating the pattern of trying to make themselves feel better by helping those around them.

Moving forwards: The Angel-Prisoner needs to establish boundaries and learn that looking after themselves *first* is the most selfless thing they can do. That way, they're self-sufficient and don't become someone else's problem. Just as importantly, they can only give what they have - so keeping their resources topped up has to be a worthwhile priority.

THE ARCHITECT

ARCHITECTS are practical, logical and efficient - and with their superlative organisational skills, they can be relied upon to 'get the job done'. Systems and processes are wonderfully useful tools to the Architect and before they start any new endeavour, they'll carefully plan each step - down to the minutest detail - to avoid problems further down the line.

What can help the ARCHITECT: Their calm and efficient nature means everyone needs an Architect on the team – so they're never short of work. However, they would do well to apply their planning skills to not only doing a 'great job' - but also to building a database of connections. After all, it's relationships that are key to long term employment and business success.

The trap that could undermine the ARCHITECT: An over-reliance on the systems and processes the Architect already has in place can prevent them from making new discoveries. Additionally, with so many other people relying on them to get things done, there's a danger of the Architect failing to take the necessary time out to simply enjoy life.

Three 'Insight Questions' for Architects:

1. Are you making enough time to investigate new ways of doing things?

2. What can you delegate to others so that you have more time for you?

3. How can you design a better work/life balance – and diarise time for relaxation and creativity, so that you get to enjoy life more?

ARCHITECT GLOBAL ROLE: PLANNING

Architects are self-contained individuals whose highly prized organisational skills ensure that they always manage to remain calm in a crisis. They know - and have always known - that their role is to organise.

Preferring to rely on the **facts** when it comes to taking decisions, wise Architects always do their homework (including any 'fringe' research) in plenty of time - as they hate the very idea of being caught out.

Priding themselves on systems, processes and frameworks, Architects know that great success comes from great planning. While they recognise that 'change happens', they also leave as little to chance as is practically possible.

Goals, action plans, diaries - these are the tools of the Architect who loves nothing more than designing and using charts and measurement systems to help turn other people's ideas into practical reality.

Aware that they're not always seen as the most 'fun' person on the team - not least because they're unafraid to play Devil's Advocate - Architects nonetheless pride themselves on quietly knowing that things happen **because** of them.

Less flamboyant than many of their counterparts, Architects choose to fit in, rather than stand out. They understand that knowledge and power often come from being free to observe from the wings - rather than being centre stage. While they may not be the Alpha male or female, over time Architects often become the lynchpin of the office (or project). They always somehow seem to have the answers - and if they don't, they'll roll up their sleeves and work it out. They enjoy the challenge of the puzzle.

It's not so much that Architects avoid conflict because they don't like it per se - it's more a case of them really not seeing the point of over-heated emotions. After all, why waste time arguing when you could actually be getting on with building something?

Erring on the side of caution and unlikely - ever - to get swept away on a wave of over-enthusiasm, Architects play nicely. They don't see the point of creating enemies and often soothe difficult (or egotistical) colleagues by pointing out that 'what's right' is far more important than 'who's right'.

In order to thrive, Architects need to ensure that everyone's goals are neatly aligned and learn how to win over the hearts and minds of everyone within the team.

Architects recognise that the best gift they can give the world is to attend to their own needs first - not in a selfish way, but out of a distaste at the thought of being a burden to others. Self-sufficiency is much prized by Architects.

In general, Architects prefer to fit in, rather than stand out. They know the rules - and while they don't so much judge others for not conforming, they **will** notice (and make a mental note for the future). They also quietly believe that society's 'rules' - spoken or otherwise - exist in order to make it better for everyone.

Architects are over-archingly polite and are respectful of their own and others' boundaries. They take this attitude through everything in life. Architects don't drive excessively fast, play their music too loudly (and risk annoying the people around them) or queue jump.

Having said that, they'll do what it takes to cater for their own needs too - which is why when they're on holiday, they're happy to get up early to 'bag' their preferred sun-bed while everyone else is still sleeping off 'the night before'.

Rarely do Architects get drunk - they prefer to remain in control.

KEY ROLES: Planner, Orchestrator, Systems Designer

KEY BELIEF: "I organise ideas into practical reality"

KEY LESSON: Enjoying today while planning for tomorrow

KEY STRENGTH: Logic

KEY DESIRE: Order

ARCHITECT PERSONAL DRIVE: ORCHESTRATING

Personal integrity is important to Architects and they're very uncomfortable if for some reason, they're not able to follow through on a promise. Similarly, punctuality is important to them - and they deem it disrespectful if someone turns up late for an appointment. Architects respect others - especially their time - and expect others to show respect for them.

With their 'live and let live' attitude - Architects like to be in control of themselves and their own lives. They are also particularly mindful of not intruding into other people's personal zones. And this is doubly true when emotions are involved.

Equally uncomfortable with over-emotionality, Architects tend to avoid people when they're in some kind of emotional pain or grief. This isn't actually because they're cold and unfeeling, it's more about not wanting to intrude at a 'difficult time'. However, ask an Architect for practical help, and they'll deliver.

When Architects design systems to serve people, everyone's life becomes easier...

Uncomfortable with over-generosity and over-inflated gratitude, Architects do nonetheless like their efforts to be acknowledged and appreciated.

They also like to be recognised for their knowledge and educational prowess - and it's not uncommon for Architects to have 'letters' after their name. Whatever their subject, Architects demand evidence and only really feel comfortable when there's ***proof***.

Scientific and logical in their approach, Architects enjoy learning and expect to 'build' their knowledge according to an already proven framework or formula. Less likely to make 'discoveries' of their own or come up with entrepreneurial new ideas, Architects are particularly good at following proven systems created by others.

For this reason, should they choose to set up in business for themselves (and this is only likely to happen when they've either built up a nest egg or received a large unexpected sum through an inheritance or a redundancy package), Architects are most likely to buy into a proven franchise model. Knowing that all they need do to make money is to follow a tried-and-tested system enables the Architect to sleep well at night.

ARCHITECT: RELATIONSHIP WITH MONEY

Usually savers from a very young age, Architects love nothing more than being self-sufficient. More comfortable than all the other 'Money Types' with the idea of budgeting, putting money to one side for old age and planning both their present and their future; Architects do all they can to remove any element of financial surprise.

Architects are those quiet types who live relatively modestly, but who are able to retire young because they've quietly been building a nest egg right from the outset. Read about a person who lives in a 'normal' house and drives a regular car but who is actually a millionaire and you can bet your bottom dollar that he or she is an Architect.

With a constant eye on the future, Architects find it easy to 'go without' in the present, in order to turn their goals into reality in the future. Indeed, they'll actually find it fun. They keep their plans to themselves and tend not to talk about their aspirations.

Why?

In their self-sufficiency, Architects know that before they start **anything**, they need to do all the necessary research and due diligence. They're happy to consult specialists-in-their-field for advice before starting to turn their plan into reality. So, why bother wasting time discussing their objectives with people who have no relevant expertise or experience to share?

Smart Architects are also aware that others - either through jealousy or a misguided desire to help them avoid disappointment - may try to pour cold water on their plans. And while they may not know why, Architects just 'get' that talking and talking about stuff somehow depletes the energy required to get things **done**.

When a milestone is achieved, Architects celebrate - but in a fairly low key way. Expect an invitation but don't be surprised when the only glass of champagne you get is for the official 'toast'. After all, Architects aren't comfortable with vulgar and ostentatious displays of wealth.

Generally speaking, Architects dislike debt - and while they might accept a mortgage as part of 'what needs to be done' to get on the property ladder, they'll do all they can to pay off the mortgage early, recognising that even small monthly over-payments can lead to big savings down the line.

Wherever possible, Architects avoid borrowing, unless there's a very sound commercial reason - like spreading payments over time at zero interest (which leaves more available each month to either save or pay down the mortgage.)

Architects are also good at checking that they're always getting the 'best deal' available. They're the ones who, each year, check comparison sites for utility, insurance and mobile phone costs. They absolutely believe that a 'penny saved is a penny earned'.

Right from when they were young children, Architects have a strong sense of their own boundaries - especially when it comes to money. They have no difficulty in politely saying 'no' (rather than 'yes') as an immediate response to a request for financial assistance - and they recognise that the one person for whom they must take responsibility is **themselves**.

In their later years, when they've built up more than enough wealth for their own needs, they'll help out their children - to an extent. They'll be happy to gift their children a deposit for a house (seeing that as a sensible investment) and they also believe in paying for education (again, because it's a good investment). Helping their children understand the difference between 'spending' and 'saving' is important - and as the conversations become more sophisticated, the lessons expand to include 'investing' and the benefits of 'compound interest'.

Architects recognise that their unique ability to take care of the detail ensures that life remains safe and secure for everyone in their orbit - and not just for themselves.

However, Architects definitely won't spoil their children and instead encourage them to earn their pocket money from a relatively young age, particularly when it comes to spending on clothes, holidays and treats. Architects want to instil their own brand of self-sufficiency in their children and while they may plan to leave a generous inheritance, they'd be appalled at the idea of their offspring 'expecting it' or worse, squandering it.

Understanding their own value, Architects can often end up earning more than their peers, purely because when it comes to negotiating their own pay package, they're able to rationally set out what cost benefits they bring to an organisation. They'll have also taken the trouble to find out what others - who work for an organisation's competitors - are paid.

Ideal careers for Architects

Law | Project Management | Technology

Finance | Security | Product Design | Military

Transport | Compliance | Manufacturing

Changes in the law - especially with regard to financial matters - rarely escape the Architect, who constantly has his or her finger on the pulse of what's happening in the world of finance. While others might miss the opportunities offered by workplace pension schemes for example - even dismissing such things as irrelevant - the Architect knows that every single advantage (however small) will add to incremental growth.

And reliable incremental growth makes them happy.

Cautious and often somewhat risk averse, Architects are self-determining individuals who make the time and take the trouble to learn how to create as stress-free a life as possible. In his world famous book *"The 7 Habits of Highly Effective People"*, Stephen Covey writes a whole chapter about 'Beginning with the End in Mind' - something that comes very naturally to Architects. Indeed, it's almost as though they were born pre-programmed with the book - as 'efficiency' and 'effectiveness' run through the Architect like a stick of fairground rock.

Architects already have it pretty well sussed when it comes to making money - indeed, they're the ones who often start building a nest egg from the day they receive their first pay packet. Saving is something that's come naturally to them and this is a habit they'll have first put in place when they were young children. They value and practice balance - budgeting to enjoy life now but also ensuring that they have more than enough stashed away for both a rainy day *and* old age.

Often - but not always - more comfortable when they're in an employed position with an organisation large enough to offer them plenty of security (and those all important salary and pension benefits) they are nevertheless wise enough to take care of their *own* finances from the outset. They usually have several baskets in which they keep their hard-earned money - after all, mitigating risk is one of their mantras.

For this reason, the Architect is the most likely of all the 'Money Types' to save a sensible portion of their salary in order to get in on the investment game sooner rather than later - whether that's through the stock market, property or even other people working for you. After all, as Albert Einstein purportedly said, "Compound interest is the most powerful force in the Universe".

The Architect's aim is to create sufficient passive income to cover their living costs (both now and in the future) as soon as possible. With that in place, not only do they feel truly secure - but they also enjoy the freedom of being able to *choose* whether or not to continue working.

And it's this 'choice point' that gives the Architect the scope to do something completely different - just for the fun of it. And when the Architect approaches business - or the world of employment - for 'fun' rather than 'necessity', magic very often happens.

It's time to join forces with others...

While all of us can achieve a certain amount on our own, it's when we collaborate with others, that *big* things can happen. The Architect will particularly thrive in a business partnership with both a Magician and a Joker. The entrepreneurial Magician has an uncanny ability to spot opportunities and to create the solutions to the problems people didn't always even know they had. The Joker, who focuses on relationships, is able to connect those ideas with the world. The Architect relishes putting the plan in place to turn all that 'talk' into reality. Without the Architect, the Magician and Joker simply won't fulfil their potential - and the wise ones know it.

To make this kind of business partnership work though, there needs to be mutual respect and a clear division of who's in charge of what.

As the Architect's second 'career' takes off and their assets grow and possibly become more complicated, they **may** choose to bring in someone to oversee it all for them. Of course, they'll keep a watchful eye on everything - but if they're smart enough, they'll recognise the value of paying for **specialist** expertise. After all, at this level, there are likely to be things for which the Architect needs specific advice - and they're not the kind of person who enjoys being tripped up by the unexpected.

How to have difficult money conversations at home

Architects love everything to be streamlined and organised. They often have neat little folders containing date-sorted paperwork - and usually they'll also have a spreadsheet which itemises **everything**. What they don't always see is that what is just 'logical and orderly' for an Architect can feel 'judgemental and suffocating' to anyone else. Architects enjoy conversations about money - and are bewildered that other people don't seem so keen (they have no idea that their approach can be somewhat off-putting). Indeed, Architects can get so bogged down in the fine detail that they lose sight of the dreams and ambitions they and their romantic partners both had at the outset. Inviting the Architect to take care of file keeping and organising financial conversations - while their partner takes the lead in reminding both parties about the bigger picture is often a neat solution.

When it comes to talking about money in business

The Architect relishes talking about money in business and they like nothing more than having their finger on the financial pulse. They don't just look at how much money the business is making, but they'll focus - a lot - **on costs and how money can be saved**. They are disinclined to take risks with the company's cash and will only sanction expansion when they're comfortable that firstly, there are sufficient reserves in the bank and secondly, that there is a robust business plan in place. They're more inclined to question what could go wrong - and so find themselves, sometimes unfairly, being accused of raining on everyone else's parade. Wise people in business recognise that having someone play 'devil's advocate' when it comes to big decisions ensures that everyone gets to keep a roof over their heads in the long term. In this case, there's no-one better for the role of devil's advocate than the Architect.

The Architect's attitude to financial risk

Planners by nature, Architects really don't like surprises and they do all they can to learn from others' mistakes - as well as their successes. Prudent and hard working, they're the people who've understood from an early age that **saving** brings peace of mind - and that by harnessing the magic of 'compound interest', they can make their money work even harder. They don't like having all their eggs in one basket and pride themselves on having thought of everything. Quick to question - and to dive deep into the detail - Architects are happy to leave everything to the 'experts', but only once they're fully satisfied that no stone has been left unturned.

How to persuade or sell to the Architect

The Architect likes to ask detailed - often **very detailed** - questions so that they're not likely to be met with any unexpected, unpleasant surprises. They're acutely aware of 'value for money' and while they'll pay handsomely for something if they value it, they need to see plenty of evidence that they're making a smart decision.

Printed literature needs to focus on facts - preferably backed up with plenty of proven evidence, case studies and testimonials.

ARCHITECTS AT WORK: As the boss

Architect bosses always plan very carefully for their team's success and they carefully chunk everything down into manageable goals. They create frameworks and processes - which are carefully thought out and leave no room for confusion. They make sure that the job gets done, on time and within budget. People within their team - together with clients and suppliers - all know that the Architect can be relied upon to keep his or her word, and that they'll fulfil their commitments and hit their deadlines.

Finding surprises unpleasant, they also take great care to familiarise themselves with all aspects of the task in hand, so that they know where any obstacles are likely to occur - and how best to avoid or repair them, with the minimum of fuss.

More comfortable with systems and processes than they are with people, Architects do recognise that it's vital to get the right people in the right roles. Perhaps predictably, Architects write out very precise job descriptions, ask each candidate the same set of questions and always follow up on references.

Good at delegating responsibility to others, Architects recognise that careful planning is required. They can be likened to an orchestra's conductor - bringing in the right people at the right time, to achieve a successful outcome.

Perhaps not the most stirring, inspiring or eloquent of communicators, Architects nevertheless are clear - and everyone in their team is left in no doubt as to what's expected of them. In order to achieve such feats of organisation, Architects first describe what overall outcome is required and then allocate tasks to each individual team member. They often use SMART (Specific, Measurable, Achievable, Realistic and Timed) terminology, just to ensure that no-one is left in any doubt as to what's expected.

Architects also put plenty of measurement systems in place - so that activities, people and outcomes can be monitored. They have a firm belief that 'what gets measured, gets done'. Sophisticated Architects take it up a level, agreeing with Robin Sharma of "*The Monk Who Sold His Ferrari*" fame who pointed out that 'what gets measured, gets ***improved***'.

Firm and fair, Architects run their organisations like clockwork and love nothing more than being in charge of repeatable processes that can reliably put food on the table. And if they can spot ways to make incremental improvements, they'll do so - but only when they've been examined from every angle and ***proven***. After all, Architects never leave any room for error.

As managers & colleagues

Architects who work within an organisation are those stalwarts who can always be relied upon to get the job done properly. They require little management - providing they're given clear guidelines as to what's expected from them at the outset. Fastidious and detail-focused, Architects always double check their work to ensure that potential errors are avoided. They hate being 'caught out'.

They enjoy responsibility and are good at supervising others because everyone in the team knows where they stand and what role they must fulfil. Often the Architect will create systems and processes for others to follow, simply to improve efficiency and remove the likelihood of error.

Preferring to work in calm environments where they can just get on with the 'job in hand', Architects don't thrive particularly well with overly emotional people or under stress. Indeed, they like to anticipate and plan for potential problems long before they arise - and in all likelihood will already have a procedure that can be followed in such circumstances.

Architects expect to work for the hours they're paid - and to be paid for the hours they work. While they will go the extra mile in a true emergency, they don't agree with the majority who take work home as a matter of course. They believe that if you're regularly having to work outside your paid hours then there's something wrong: either you're not up to the job or your employer is exploiting you.

Before stepping in to help colleagues, Architects first make sure that all their own duties have been fulfilled. They understand that they're responsible for their particular 'cog' in the system and that leaving their 'station' to help someone else could result in disaster down the line for everyone.

While they're not great at handling people's emotional issues (believing that everyone should leave matters that are not work-related at the 'door' when they arrive in the morning), Architects are good at unravelling technology issues. Having problems with emails or the printer? Call in the Architect - and remember to thank them properly afterwards (but don't gush, it embarrasses them).

ARCHITECT: UNDERSTANDING THE SHADOW

In Jungian psychology, the 'shadow' refers to the 'unknown' or unconscious dark side of the personality which the ego does not recognise within itself (even if it's pretty obvious to everyone else!). It could even be said that until we identify and then 'own' our shadow aspect, it'll keep us trapped in self-sabotaging and self-defeating patterns. Just as unpalatably, the 'shadow' is the unowned part of us that manipulates others.

If it's any consolation, we all have a 'shadow'.

For the Architect, the shadow plays out through close-mindedness and self-righteousness. Those who just don't 'get' the Architect will tend to see them as humourless nitpickers who always see the glass as half empty.

Rarely charismatic, Architects at their worst can come across as cold, colourless and without emotion. Many will consider them boring, whereas the Architect him or herself will instead pride themselves on being a 'safe pair of hands'.

Shadow Architects can be unbearably inflexible. Once a decision has been made, they expect everyone to stick to the plan, even if new information suggests that **adapting** the original plan would be beneficial. Anyone altering plans at the last minute earns a reputation among Architects for being 'flaky' - and in their eyes, little could be more damning.

Gifted with a supremely stubborn streak - which tends to come to the fore under stress, Architects particularly dig their heals in when it comes to speed. To be in their comfort zone, they like to be slow and methodical. Being rushed by others who are in a panic is of particular irritation. In such circumstances, Architects find themselves wondering why everyone else can't just be more like them and think things through **first**. Shadow Architects can be exacting, judgmental and unblinkingly non-understanding when it comes to what makes people tick. It's not that they mean to be cruel, but they just can't abide 'drama' or understand how or why people manage to get themselves into so many pickles.

While Architects are generally good at looking after their physical health - eating comparatively well and taking regular exercise - it's a completely different story when it comes to their emotional and spiritual health.

Their need for evidence and their dependence on logic means that they often find it hard to comprehend people who prefer to be led by their heart. Shadow Architects can be dismissive of them - and their clinically logical arguments don't always help them win friends. Disdainful of 'emotionality', Shadow Architects can pride themselves on being able to shut down their emotions, believing that this is a strength. In the short term, it may be - but emotions that are suppressed often leak out later in life, often through illness.

Shadow Architects are painstakingly organised (they'll be the ones whose kitchen cupboards are stocked with rows and rows of neatly stacked tins in alphabetical order) and they're generally easily distressed when presented with mess.

It has to be said that Shadow Architects can be controlling - and their compulsion to follow the rules can make it difficult for the people accompanying them on life's journey. Shadow Architects can grow to believe that their way, **their logical way,** is the only way. Woe betide anyone who argues with them, unless they come armed with irrefutable evidence.

Often preferring their own company, Shadow Architects sometimes follow the rules to such an extent that they're, well, boring. After all, it's our differences, peculiarities and gifts that make us interesting. Shadow Architects are more comfortable when they can hide in plain view.

Shadow Architects can be accused of being dogmatic - and they love to go over and over whatever it is that's currently bothering them, in an attempt to ensure that no morsel remains unturned. While this provides them with reassurance (and if they're smart, they learn from this introspection and apply their new knowledge in their future endeavours) the people around them quickly grow sick and tired of hearing the same thing over and over again, as if on a loop.

Finally, Shadow Architects often simply aren't great sharers. Rather than splitting a bill equally at a restaurant, they'll be the ones with the calculator - carefully working out who ate what. Similarly at the bar, rather than stand their round, they're more likely to refuse drinks from others (so as not to be in their debt) but they'll prefer to buy their own too, so that they can retain control of the purse strings. Shadow Architects often find it difficult to trust anyone other than themselves.

How the Architect can self-sabotage

The Architect's seeming inability to understand that while logic may be safe, it's **emotions that persuade** - which can lead to a repeated lack of 'buy-in' from other people holding the purse strings.

What the Architect deeply believes about themselves

Some deeply-held beliefs are positive while others emanate from the shadows. Intriguingly, these beliefs are often a variation on the same theme:

Light Belief: "I truly DO love nothing more than creating order out of chaos and streamlining things so that they run efficiently."

Shadow Belief: "I can't trust other people."

ARCHITECT: HOW THEY APPROACH LIFE

in all relationships, the careful, cautious and practical Architect has learned from the outset to protect themselves and their boundaries - choosing what they want and leading their own lives, rather than being an integral part in other people's. They have no difficulty with the word 'no'.

Architects never allow themselves to get caught on the hop - and anyone issuing either an invitation or a request to an Architect will be met by the same response: "I'll give it some consideration and get back to you." This strategy enables them to find a way to refuse unwanted invitations without causing offence and also prevents them from having any sense of obligation to help others. If they later decide that an invitation is suitable, they will graciously accept. Similarly, if after consideration they decide that they do indeed have the personal resources to help someone else, there's a chance that they will. But first, they'll want to satisfy themselves that their help will be used wisely and that it won't lead to further obligation.

When Architects make the decision to commit to another - whether in marriage, with their children, in a business or in a voluntary capacity - they do so with a rare degree of thoroughness. And it's because they know that they take commitment seriously that they're very wary of getting involved in the first place. Anyone enjoying any kind of relationship with an Architect must first have won their respect and loyalty. With these in place, the Architect reciprocates if not whole-heartedly, then certainly whole-mindedly.

ARCHITECT: AS A ROMANTIC PARTNER

Architects aren't renowned for being the most romantic of people - however, they have high integrity and when they make a commitment, they give it their all. Architects like things done properly and many of them choose to get married. Their brides-to-be can expect a proper engagement ring but it most definitely won't be flashy. Having said that, any diamonds will at least be real. Similarly, Architect brides like things to be done tastefully, but they'd rather save for a deposit for a home (which they'd see as an investment) than blow everything on an ostentatious wedding that's all over in a day.

Worth considering: Architects in relationships like to have a clear plan from the outset. They want to know what to expect - and by when. They like to know which party will be responsible for what, and Architects expect everyone to keep their side of the bargain. Architects are loyal and dependable but the very routines that they like because they provide security can lead to things becoming just, well a bit boring.

Two Architects in one marriage need to learn to let their hair down on occasion and just have some fun (even if they have to plan for it!). Architects coupled with a Magician, Joker or Angel bring organised balance to what could otherwise be a chaotic party. However, if partnered with a Pharaoh or Prisoner they need to take care that things don't just become darkly intense. A battle for power with a Pharaoh leads to the wrong kind of excitement for an Architect while a relationship with a dyed-in-the-wool Prisoner can give rise to depression.

How Architects handle money in a relationship

Architects are often the ones who look after the money within the household. With their penchant for spreadsheets and their love of organisation and filing, they're able to account for every penny - and delight in living according to a budget. Architects don't like surprises and they particularly don't like financial surprises of the unwanted kind. Partners who have sufficient self-worth are usually perfectly content to give the Architect free rein with the household finances (after all, it's just a boring job off their own list). However, partners who have issues with authority or their own self-esteem can misunderstand the Architect's intentions. When an Architect requests monthly expenditure receipts, partners can feel controlled, monitored and belittled. While the Architect is merely trying to **organise** their finances, their partners can feel that they're being made to **justify** what they've spent. Arguments can often ensue - much to the Architect's complete bewilderment.

ARCHITECT: AS A PARENT

Architects take parenting seriously. They set the rules for the family and expect their children to abide by them. Often quite strict, they are also scrupulously fair and their children generally prosper because they feel secure. Architects have no doubt where their responsibilities lie - and there's no doubt that there will always be food on the table and a roof overhead. Architect parents value education highly and are prepared to invest in it accordingly. Their children are expected to work hard and get good results. As well as their school studies, Architect parents will do what they can to broaden their children's horizons - taking them on educational trips, teaching them about money and playing instructive board games (such as Monopoly) with them. Architect parents enjoy spending time with their children and get involved with their hobbies and pet projects. Family time is important - eating around the table together, going on holiday together (camping or self-catering rather than swanky hotels) and generally sharing experiences together. While they remain involved in their children's lives when they become adults, Architects expect their children to be completely self-sufficient. If they're in a position to do so, they may contribute to a wedding or a house deposit but they'd much rather *offer* than be asked.

Worth considering: While children are reassured by boundaries and rules, they can only truly blossom when their unique gifts are recognised, developed and appreciated. Wise Architects know that children don't have to follow in their parents' footsteps to live worthy and fulfilling lives.

ARCHITECT: AS A CHILD

Architect children are sensible and often 'older than their years'. They understand and abide by the rules, do well at school (and beyond) and rarely give their parents much trouble. However, the parents of an Architect child know that it's good for them to stretch themselves and to step out of their comfort zones - physically, intellectually and emotionally. Likely to go to University, Architect children tend to get good jobs which pay well. They save from a young age and often astound the adults around them by how much they've managed to amass. Architect children expect to look after their parents as they age - and family remains important to them throughout their lives.

Worth considering: Architect children can fall into the trap of thinking that they're only loved and accepted because they tow the family line - it can be very empowering for them to learn that even if they break the rules on occasion, the love of their parents remains true and unconditional.

ARCHITECT: HOW THEY RELATE TO TIME

Architects always have sufficient time because they plan everything so meticulously. They fulfil their own duties and obligations first and then choose how to spend their time after that - usually with family or pursuing their hobbies. They value punctuality and see it as a sign of respect - and take a dim view of people who don't behave similarly. Whenever they plan for a journey, they always anticipate the possibility of a delay and allow sufficient contingency time. They find tales of people missing a plane because they arrived late at an airport completely perplexing.

How the Architect breaches boundaries around time

The Architect can waste time by fiddling with endless detail - but ignoring the overall purpose behind the 'bigger picture'.

ARCHITECT: WHAT THEY WEAR

Architects tend to be practical and like to dress comfortably - and above all, they like to fit in. Inclined to keep fit and take care of themselves physically, Architects wear their clothes well. They often choose colour rather than monochrome black and white - but opt for natural 'muted' shades, coupled with navy and beige. Architects tend to buy good quality clothing but they avoid excessively expensive designer labels, believing them to be unnecessarily showy. Ostentatious displays of wealth really don't sit well with Architects. And while they may have a multi-functional sports watch that isn't cheap, it definitely won't be diamond encrusted. Before arriving anywhere, they make sure to both know the dress code - and to follow it. Their shoes (and cars) are clean and polished.

HOW OTHER - HIGH SCORING - 'MONEY TYPES' CAN INFLUENCE THE ARCHITECT

Architect - Pharaoh:

This individual has the ability to lead - and adopts a very pragmatic and logical approach. They see BIG projects through to fruition by creating a tight framework and measurable action plan for others to follow. Little phases them and whatever they set out to achieve, they achieve comfortably and with a little fanfare.

Watch out for: The Architect-Pharaoh can come across as very serious and dogmatic, which might be off-putting for some people and downright scary for others. They need to know that when people are intimidated, they don't perform at their best.

Moving forwards: The Architect-Pharaoh needs to learn that great projects are achieved through people - and work out how best to nurture them.

Architect - Magician:

Able to hold the 'vision', this individual is also capable of simultaneously focusing on the finer detail to make stuff happen. The Architect-Magician particularly enjoys implementing **other people's** projects and prefers to work for a larger organisation than for themselves in a freelance capacity.

Watch out for: The Architect-Magician can have a tendency to focus on the finer detail while missing the 'bigger picture' completely.

Moving forwards: The Architect-Magician needs to learn to consistently keep the bigger picture in mind in order to achieve the desired outcome. This approach will also help them to remember **why** they're doing what they're doing.

Architect - Joker:

A natural team leader, this individual often manages to turn what can seem mundane, into something much more fun. The Architect-Joker is not only great at organising things so that they go to plan - but they also ensure that the team is acknowledged and that all successes are celebrated.

Watch out for: This individual needs to understand that the people they're in business with just love it when they're the centre of the Architect-Joker's attention - but can feel rejected and resentful when that attention is directed elsewhere.

Moving forwards: The Architect-Joker needs to recognise that successful leaders *share the credit but take the blame*.

Architect - Angel:

This individual is naturally able to implement frameworks and plans in place to make the world a better place. The Angel aspect introduces intuition and compassion, which can soften the Architect's logic and pragmatism - which means that people will take more kindly to the Architect-Angel's management style.

Watch out for: When this individual is overwhelmed and stressed by the sheer amount on their plate, those around them are likely to grow anxious that the Architect-Angel is out of their depth - or feel guilty for not being able to do more to help. They would do well to remember that panic can be contagious.

Moving forwards: The Architect-Angel needs to learn to inspire themselves and others by shining the light on how the work *everyone* is doing contributes to the bigger picture. This can be done easily by ensuring that project milestones are celebrated.

Architect - Prisoner:

This individual is able to see what *isn't* working and what most definitely needs to be fixed. Fuelled by a heady mixture of injustice and determination to put 'wrongs' right, they put a careful plan in place to fight for those causes in which they passionately believe.

Watch out for: Obsessional fighting for what seems like a 'worthy cause' can lead to others perceiving the Architect-Prisoner as difficult, angry or judgemental. They also have a tendency to endlessly repeat - as if on a loop and to anyone who'll listen - their list of woes and injustices. Draining people's energy and goodwill, this individual can find themselves being ostracised - which results in them feeling increasingly hard-done-by.

Moving forwards: The Architect-Prisoner needs to learn how to keep others on side - by inspiring them with a positive vision. They would also do well to recognise that people are more inclined to want to fight *for* - rather than *against* - something.

THE PRISONER

PRISONERS often feel trapped. Whatever they do, it feels as though they're never going to be able to break free from where they are now. However, by doing some personal development work they can begin to understand their subconscious patterns and behaviours - and learn how to let go of their limiting beliefs. In this way, Prisoners can liberate themselves - and go on to enjoy happier and more prosperous lives.

What can help the PRISONER: Rather than fighting or simply giving up, Prisoners need to understand that their current problems are actually an invitation to see that they **deserve better**. Learning through others who've overcome similar experiences can inspire the Prisoner to try doing things differently.

The trap that could undermine the PRISONER: It's tempting for Prisoners to classify themselves as victims – and become attached to their 'story'. While they may get the sympathy of everyone around them in the short term, playing the victim card will however, always keep them stuck with the life they don't want in the long term.

Three 'Insight Questions' for Prisoners:

1. What is the story that you continually replay to yourself and others?

2. What beliefs do you have – possibly from your family and friends – that are keeping you stuck in an unhelpful way of thinking?

3. Who can help you on your journey to freedom?

PRISONER GLOBAL ROLE: LIBERATOR

Despite their name, prisoners actually bring a whole lot to the party. Their whole reason for being is to observe what **isn't** working at a personal level - and to fix it.

Prisoners often get a bad rap as being 'whinging victims' who avoid taking responsibility. While this can be true for Prisoners operating in their shadow (more on that later), when they're playing to their strengths, it's a whole different story.

With their focus on freedom - which itself is one of the highest goals of enlightenment! - Prisoners propel us forwards, into expansion and growth. After all, isn't it true that those things we aspire to at one point in our lives often go on to become the things that stifle us as we continue on our journey? For example, as children, we may have longed for a job delivering newspapers early in the morning, just so we could have a little pocket money of our own and have at least a taste of independence. But ask an adult if they'd be happy to still have the same 'job' - and they'd be horrified.

It could be said then, that the Prisoner gives us a sense of growth - and maybe ambition too. But more importantly, the Prisoner invites us to exercise our free will with **choice**.

When we live with choice, we're free - and the Prisoner is happy.

Prisoners are great judges - comparing themselves and their lot with everyone around them. But if they only realised that their views are skewed, they would be relieved - and much happier.

Prisoners don't understand that they're never comparing 'like for like' because they only keep score at a superficial level. Instead, they feel bitter and resentful if someone has more money than they do, or has a better job. Or they're unhappy that someone else is slimmer or more muscle-bound than they are. Or they fear that someone else is better educated or that their house is bigger. The list goes on and on - with the focus solely being on what they **don't** have.

But the truth is that there are a myriad of scales for just about everything - and there will always be some people with more and some with less.

Sometimes the Prisoner has to dig just a little deeper to unearth their precious gifts - but when they do, it's like finding gold.

In order to thrive, Prisoners need to take back their personal power and learn to align their goals with other people's aspirations. When they do, magic happens.

Often people find themselves becoming Prisoners either because of the hand that life has dealt them - or because of a difficult childhood (or possibly both - after all, one thing often leads to another.)

However, when Prisoners heed the comment from America's 'top ideas man' and advertising guru Stanley Arnold, who says that 'Every problem contains within itself the seeds of its own solution', they can rest assured. There is *hope* - however bleak their present or past. In many cases, Prisoners find that as adults, the majority of their problems in life revolve around money. Of course, it's all too easy to blame money itself - but money is merely the mirror. When Prisoners improve their relationship with ***themselves***, their relationship with money rapidly improves too and they go on to prosper - both financially and in terms of their own happiness.

KEY ROLES: Observer, Advocate, Enforcer

KEY BELIEF: "I can see what isn't working and what needs to change"

KEY LESSON: Approaching life with optimism and gratitude

KEY STRENGTH: Endurance

KEY DESIRE: Justice

PRISONER PERSONAL DRIVE: FREEDOM

Prisoners are very much in touch with their emotions - particularly those that make them feel uncomfortable. Sadly, most people try to ignore any feelings of emotional malaise - either by putting on a brave face, or by medicating themselves with alcohol, drugs, sex, shopping - anything to take the 'edge off'.

But the Prisoner doesn't want to make other people's life difficult - on the contrary, he or she is only trying to get the attention of the people around them and to invite everyone to find a **better way**. And rest assured, there **always** is a better way.

> *When Prisoners learn to take personal responsibility for themselves and their lives, they become unstoppable. They become the heroes and heroines who inspire others.*

All it takes is a **decision** to leave victimhood behind and to choose to step into one's power. The change occurs in an instant - and always begins on the inner planes. Later (and how much later depends on the actions one takes) the inner change is reflected in one's outer landscape.

Sooner or later, most Prisoners choose to follow a path of personal development. Before they begin, they fear being judged as a failure (which is of course a projection of their own thoughts). Later, they begin to realise that they've given themselves the greatest gift of all: Knowledge and understanding of the self. And as this in turn develops, it goes on to become 'love of self' at the highest level. The ego is at first embraced and then transcended and a permanent higher state of being ensues.

Never underestimate the commitment and depth of the journey to true self - but know too, that the ultimate prize is of such value, it has no price.

PRISONER: RELATIONSHIP WITH MONEY

Prisoners have a difficult relationship with money - often finding that there just isn't **enough** of it. Whatever does come in seems to go straight back out again - on bills. And if by any happy chance, there is a windfall - whether it's a tax rebate, an inheritance or a pay rise, it always seems to be swiftly followed by some kind of disaster which costs even more.

Little wonder that Prisoners can find themselves losing heart.

When the pattern repeats - and it so often does, the Prisoner can begin to feel that they're being victimised in some strange way by 'Money' - as though there is 'something out there' that is trying to punish them in some way.

Of course, this simply isn't true, but no-one can really blame the Prisoner for feeling this way. Money isn't **causing** the problem - but the lack of reliable money in the Prisoner's life is a **symptom**, reflecting their own troubled emotional state, coupled with their deep belief that they are unworthy.

Prisoners facing an almost permanent struggle with money can find themselves experiencing a kind of 'battle fatigue', in which they're just not able to go on.

Feeling hopeless, some just give up and believe that nothing will ever change in their lives. Others can decide that there's no point in trying, so whatever cash does come in, they simply fritter away on anything that helps them feel better in the moment. Little do they realise that they're just perpetuating their own pain.

The Prisoner is actually being delivered an invitation: Wake Up!

Once Prisoners recognise that it's **their way of thinking** that's keeping them stuck, they're set free. Everything in our outer world is a reflection of what's going on internally for us. So, when Prisoners change their inner thought patterns, the outer world shifts too.

Easy to say, not always as easy to do. However, when Prisoners choose to examine their lives and to take responsibility for where they are **now**, they start to take their own power back. While we may not have chosen everything that's happened to us in life, we can **choose** how we respond - and that's the key.

Prisoners have developed huge reservoirs of endurance - and when they couple this with courage, they're able to turn their financial lives around. Often remarkably quickly.

While the benefits may not be immediately obvious, Prisoners are also used to 'doing without'. Although they want much 'more', Prisoners often don't have massively high monthly outgoings, compared to other people.

This can pay huge dividends when they discover that the path to long-term financial freedom is to have monthly passive income that is higher or at least equates to monthly outgoings.

It's far easier to reach this state of financial Nirvana when regular outgoings are low - so Prisoners can suddenly find themselves at a massive advantage. What Prisoners don't always recognise is that the people they envy often have very high expenditure each month - which means that they're trapped on the treadmill of having to earn a lot of money just to make ends meet. For these people - with much higher expenditure - achieving sufficient passive income to cover their outgoings is just much more **difficult**.

Getting the money flowing into their lives, paradoxically perhaps, begins with personal healing. Money flows to people when they're living on **purpose** - and it's only when we get to live on purpose and know who we are, that we're able to love ourselves. Yes, it all sounds a bit 'woo woo' but deep down, it's Prisoners who are keeping themselves locked up in their financial prisons because for some reason, they don't believe that they **deserve** more.

> *When Prisoners discover that they're the ones holding the key to their own freedom, they're able to set themselves free.*

Perhaps because of their lower self-esteem, Prisoners can struggle when it comes to negotiating their salaries.

Sadly, until they learn to value themselves - and to see what value they bring to others - Prisoners can often end up earning less than their peers, purely because they've not felt able to ask for a raise or promotion.

Indeed, at a job interview, a Prisoner is most likely to accept whatever salary they're offered rather than negotiate.

Ideal careers for Prisoners

Advocacy | Counsellor | Union Representative

Charity Activist | Fundraising | Welfare

Prisoners find it particularly frustrating when they see a lazy colleague get promoted over their heads. They can become despondent, wondering why they aren't good enough - and rather than check in to see what they themselves need to be doing differently, they can fall into the trap of complaining or whinging. This doesn't of course endear them to anyone - and they'll likely find themselves overlooked for promotion the next time too.

Instead, Prisoners are invited to consider - as dispassionately as possible - how those around them might perceive them (especially their boss!). What are more successful colleagues doing differently? Have they taken the trouble to build a better relationship with their up-line? Are they better at promoting themselves and their achievements? Do they dress and behave in a way that's suited to the job they want, rather than the one they've already got?

Prisoners often feel that life seems to be a case of 'one step forward, two steps back' - but flip their mindset and they **can** begin to see that miracles really can happen (even if they're only small at first).

When it comes to making money, Prisoners need to know that people are generally attracted to people who are upbeat, positive and who have a 'can-do' attitude - and need to learn how to behave accordingly.

The Prisoner and Angel 'Money Types' often go hand in hand. Usually, the Prisoner has been created through the over-generosity of the Angel, whose self-worth comes from helping others. Of course, taking care of loved ones - especially family and friends - is something everyone wants to do - but Angels take it to a far greater degree, often giving to others what they don't actually have themselves. To help someone else out, they can rack up **considerable debt** - little realising just how much the interest on all those credit cards is going to cost them over the months and years to come.

No surprise then, that people who started out as Angels find themselves morphing into Prisoners over time. Bewildered, angry and resentful, Prisoners shake their fists at the Universe - blaming everyone and looking for answers outside themselves.

The invitation is for the Prisoner to start doing the 'inner work'!

Sometimes, it can help simply to shift away from self blame and for the

Prisoner to start looking out for themselves as though they were their own 'best friend'. Angels (who are destined to become Prisoners until they see the patterns that are playing out) can fall into the trap of giving and giving - but what would they say to a friend they saw doing that? Wouldn't the Angel remind that friend to take care of themselves first?

It's time for the Prisoner to shift their perspective...

Prisoners may well be relieved to know that in truth, we are **all** meant to be living in abundance - so that we can **live** out our unique purpose in this life. Often the seed of the solution lies within the problem. However long the Prisoner may have been troubled by money worries, when they **choose** to alter their approach to all things financial, things really began to shift. And quite quickly too.

Rather than run away from what they fear, Prisoners are well advised to check their bank balance **every day** (which is easily done with the banking apps that are readily available). Knowing what's going on - rather than burying one's head in the sand - means that the Prisoner is able to start taking **control** (rather than feeling like a victim!).

The next step that Prisoners come to enjoy is opening a savings account - even if they don't have much to put in it at the outset. What often keeps Prisoners stuck is that believing they have nothing, they tend to blow what little they can muster on trinkets to cheer themselves up. The purpose of opening a savings account is to prove to the Prisoner that actually, they too can amass money. It's all down to choices. So, every time they resist buying something that they previously would have bought in an attempt to make themselves feel better, the Prisoner instead should move what they would have spent into their savings account. Little by little, that savings account will start to grow - and the first £100 accumulated will feel like a massive milestone! While this might seem like the tiniest of 'acorns' at the outset, it soon switches up into something bigger - as the Prisoner starts to find it more fun to watch the savings account grow than it is to buy yet more things they don't need. Soon, that £100 becomes £1,000 and so on. It's the sense of **sovereignty over one's own destiny** that is so valuable.

Weirdly - or not, if you're into these things - once the Prisoner starts to make a 'home' for building wealth, they start to attract it from different, unexpected sources. Suddenly a better paid job will come their way, or they'll find themselves left a little money from someone who's died. Optimism and hope breeds a better way of living, as the Prisoner excitedly begins to find out.

Finally, when Prisoners drop their fear of money (and especially when they realise that they're meant to have it), they learn rapidly how to create a good **relationship** with it - nurturing it with the care and attention they historically used to give away to everyone else or fritter away in frustration.

How to have difficult money conversations at home

Prisoners tend to shy away from financial conversations because they expect to be **blamed.** In the past, they've often felt stuck - and believe that for some unfathomable reason, the Universe simply overlooks or punishes them when it comes to Money. Take care not to make a Prisoner feel bullied - instead, encourage and help them come to a place of confidence in their own abilities to create change. Help them recall what they've achieved (it doesn't have to be financial) and remind them of their innate qualities. With this gentle approach, Prisoners can sensitively be guided to a place where they're able to take personal responsibility for everything in their lives. From here, they can make amazing - and often swift - changes. Take it in baby steps - and above all, remember to reassure rather than condemn.

When it comes to talking about money in business

The Prisoner is often trapped by their fear of money - and therefore avoids either discussing it, or learning more about it. Afraid of coming across as demanding or greedy (which is often how they see people who are 'good with money') the Shadow Prisoner often asks for far less than the job is worth. In this way, they devalue both themselves and the project. Shadow Prisoners often unwittingly measure their own value with money - and because they feel that they don't have 'enough', they consequently believe that **they** are not 'enough'. This erroneous belief means that Prisoners try - with all their might - to avoid money discussions because they're aware that they'll be left feeling bad about themselves afterwards.

The Prisoner's attitude to financial risk...

Life hasn't always dealt the Prisoner a good hand - and as a result, they can feel as though there's a power bigger than themselves that is out to 'punish' them. Salvation is at hand though, when they begin to see that life shifts when they shift **their own attitudes**. The invitation is for Prisoners to step away from victimhood and to reclaim their own power. When they do, they can re-write their life stories - and inspire both themselves and others. However, those stuck in Prisoner 'mode' tend to blame everyone but themselves when things don't go the way they'd hoped - while they can be unduly quick to claim credit for success, even when it's not due.

How to persuade or sell to the Prisoner

The Prisoner likes to be heard and they pride themselves on spotting inconsistencies (they have an uncanny ability to sniff out injustice). Given their often straitened circumstances, they tend to make choices according to 'price' rather than 'quality'. Unfortunately this can mean the Prisoner ends up 'buying twice', as the cheapest option often doesn't deliver on its promise. When this happens - and it so often does to the Prisoner - they're left feeling even more aggrieved than before.

Printed literature should be easy to digest with simple-to-follow instructions.

PRISONERS AT WORK: As the boss

Prisoner bosses can fall into two camps. Those with bigger hearts can try to make life as easy as possible for those they're supervising (even if the Prisoner finds him or herself picking up the slack) or they can project their own unhappiness onto everyone else - with unhappy results. And depending on which camp they fall into, Prisoner bosses don't always get it right when it comes to motivating their teams. While most people achieve their best results through a mixture of 'carrot and stick', Prisoner bosses are either deeply uncomfortable at the prospect of wielding the stick - which means that work-shy employees are all too able to take advantage of their good nature, or they enjoy seeing other people's lives made a misery (which somehow makes them feel better about their own unhappiness) which leads to them taking a more brutal approach. Prisoner bosses aren't renowned for delivering much 'carrot'.

In owner-managed businesses, Prisoners have often already propped up the organisation with their own funds (or even by re-mortgaging their home) and can become rather bitter when people on their team don't seem grateful enough. Worse, because they're coming at life from such a place of struggle, Prisoners can end up repeating the same mistakes - until they eventually run out of funding. They then have to make some pretty harsh decisions - let people go, close the business down or go bankrupt. Rarely does it occur to them to do things differently - and rather than focusing on attracting more clients and making more money, they tend to look at how they can keep cutting costs. But cutting costs only works for so long - when there's nothing left but the bare bones, it's just a case of 'last one out, switch off the lights'.

Because of their own ongoing struggles for money on a personal basis, Prisoners rarely have enough left over at the end of the month to *invest* in their businesses. Everything ends up being done on a shoe-string. While this is a good talent to have (rather than just throwing money at everything and hoping that something will work), Prisoners have to understand that their business deserves - and needs - ongoing investment. When they stop to look back, Prisoners will come to see that in a similar way, they also have never invested sufficiently in *themselves* either, probably not believing that they were worthy of it.

Prisoner bosses do well to see that their businesses are a reflection of *them*.

As managers & colleagues

Prisoners who work for someone else need to be aware of their own boundaries - as their inherent lack of self-worth can lead to them taking up the slack for their colleagues (or people working under them) as they hate to see someone getting into trouble. They need to learn that they should only step in to help others if and when their *own* needs and duties have been fulfilled. Often it needs to be spelled out to them that they will solely be judged for the results they achieve (or don't achieve) in their own job - and that 'helping others' is not an acceptable excuse for an uncompleted task. Conversely, there are some Prisoners who are so angry at life, that they almost come across as arrogantly 'entitled' - only doing exactly what they're paid for and not a moment more. Unsurprisingly, this latter attitude doesn't endear them to anyone.

Ironically though, Prisoners - irrespective of their position at work - who have someone sick at home, will expect everyone to completely understand if they need to take time off (however suddenly). They certainly don't expect to be questioned on the matter - and take offence if they're asked to justify their whereabouts or how much time off they're having.

Prisoners who are anxious about money can end up losing the ability to stand up for themselves in the workplace - bending over backwards to keep their boss happy. But this isn't always appreciated by those in supervisory roles who recognise the difference between 'love of the job' and 'desperation'. The former wins brownie points and promotions, whereas the latter attitude keeps the employee stuck (but often they just can't see why).

Equally, Prisoners can earn a reputation for being 'prepared to stand up to management' - with others creating bullets for the Prisoner to fire. While the rest of the team may benefit from improvement in their day-to-day working practices, the Prisoner generally loses out. For sure, in the short term, they can feel proud for having 'won the battle' but in the longer term, they'll have made themselves some enemies.

PRISONER: UNDERSTANDING THE SHADOW

In Jungian psychology, the 'shadow' refers to the 'unknown' or unconscious dark side of the personality which the ego does not recognise within itself (even if it's pretty obvious to everyone else!). It could even be said that until we identify and then 'own' our shadow aspect, it'll keep us trapped in self-sabotaging and self-defeating patterns. Just as unpalatably, the 'shadow' is the unowned part of us that manipulates others.

If it's any consolation, we all have a 'shadow'.

For the Prisoner, the shadow plays out through denial, victimhood and martyrdom. These attributes are fed by crippling (although often masked) self-doubt and lack of gratitude in life. Shadow Prisoners have long been renowned for playing the victim - after all, this provides them with all the excuses they need for not taking responsibility for their own lives. Many of their sentences contain the phrase, "If only... then things would be different".

While they don't always get the good things in life, Shadow Prisoners learn to get by on other people's sympathy. It makes them feel better about themselves - if only in the moment. But sadly, other people's sympathy can keep the Prisoner stuck just where they don't want to be. How much more empowering to have someone truthfully tell you something along the lines of , "I truly believe in you, you have the ability...go and change things now!" than to hear "Yes, isn't it awful...poor you!".

Prisoners often connect with other Prisoners through their comparison about how dreadful things are. Author and medical intuitive Caroline Myss refers to this as 'woundology' - there's a kind of relief when we discover someone else who's in the same boat as we find ourselves. We're no longer alone. Someone understands us.

Unfortunately though, two shadow Prisoners are likely to keep each other locked in a jail of their own making. Now their relationship rests on them both remaining stuck. If one makes a break for it - by choosing to drop their story and create a different outcome - the other one will be left behind. No one wants to be left behind - but when we're used to getting through life by trading on our stories of woe, finding the desire and energy to change can feel virtually impossible. In this scenario, each Prisoner now has a vested interest in remaining stuck themselves - and keeping the other one stuck too (if they're to have any chance of keeping their relationship alive).

Shadow Prisoners are great story tellers. They'll tell their stories of pain, grief and injustice to anyone who'll listen. And they'll tell them again and again. They do this partly because they enjoy the brief energy 'hit' they get when other people sympathise with them and partly because for them, their identities are so tightly wound up with their stories that they have little else to discuss!

And when people get sick of hearing their stories - or they come to realise that the Shadow Prisoner has no real interest in breaking free, sooner or later they walk away. But the Shadow Prisoner doesn't understand why. And instead of reflecting, they immediately jump to the conclusion that they've been abandoned. This leaves them feeling even more victimised. And thus the pattern is set to repeat - and won't change until the Shadow Prisoner comes to understand how they themselves are contributing to their own unhappiness.

Shadow Prisoners don't just regale their stories to everyone around them, they also run them in a continuous loop in their own minds. With each re-telling, things become just a little more exaggerated and as each day passes, they feel just a little more hard done by. Their resentment levels escalate, people start avoiding them in real life and things just get tougher.

The Prisoner's shadow is often birthed early in life. Either they feel guilty for something they've done or for not being 'good enough' - or they've taken on board things that their families have told them about them not deserving more.

Some Prisoners believe that others know better than they do - and they're not always good at recognising when the people around them are effectively bullying them into believing that they're not good enough and undeserving. Other Prisoners can simply take over from the people around them - and begin to **punish themselves**. Either way, the solution is understanding and acceptance, often through the gateway of forgiveness.

Finally, some people turn into Prisoners because they have a high Angel 'Money Type' playing out in their lives. Angels love to take care of everyone else - and all too often, they use their funds to support those around them, without first making sure that they have enough for themselves. When this continues, Angels can become burned out - and feeling bitter and resentful, find themselves in a prison of their own making.

How the Prisoner can self-sabotage

The Prisoner often has a seeming inability to accept that the only way to get out of the current situation is to step up and take personal responsibility and make change happen. Failing to grasp this leads to them giving their power away by living as a 'victim of circumstance'.

What the Prisoner deeply believes about themselves

Some deeply-held beliefs are positive while others emanate from the shadows. Intriguingly, these beliefs are often a variation on the same theme:

Light Belief: "When I shine a light, I can always find a way through a problem which to others, can feel impossible."

Shadow Belief: "Blaming other people brings me relief - and sometimes even makes me happy."

PRISONER: HOW THEY APPROACH LIFE

In all relationships, the vulnerable Prisoner needs to step into their own power, while at the same time protecting themselves and their boundaries.

Prisoners do well when they choose to accept that they - and they alone - hold the keys to both their freedom and their success. When the time is right and they choose to investigate and heal their inner lives, they'll soon start to see impressive progress in the outer world.

As well as improving the relationship they have with themselves - by choosing to forgive and accept the past and create strategies for success for the future - Prisoners will also begin to see their relationships with others improve too. As a result, they'll have a better relationship with money and abundance generally.

This then leads to an 'attitude of gratitude' - and perhaps for the first time, Prisoners begin to experience just how much *joy* life truly can be. Accompanying this gratitude is a desire to share and be generous - not in a manipulative way, but with the joyful knowing that 'there's plenty more where this comes from'.

When they reach this stage, Prisoners start to trust. They trust in themselves, in other people - in the Universe!

Trust, gratitude, choice - these lead to the freedom that the Prisoner has always craved. And with freedom comes joy. The hero's or heroine's journey may have been a tough quest - but the prize, when won, makes it all worthwhile.

PRISONER: AS A ROMANTIC PARTNER

Prisoners can be tough cookies as a romantic partner. Either they fight for every little thing - or they acquiesce to everything because they don't come from a place of their own personal power. More enlightened Prisoners have been on their own inner journey - so have a greater understanding of the human condition and can thus bring a great deal of wisdom to the partnership. Because of their previous struggles - most especially with money - Prisoners aren't actually demanding of expensive gifts and trips away and are often very content with small tokens. More than anyone, Prisoners truly understand that it's the 'thought that counts'.

Worth considering: Prisoners aren't great at planning for the future - especially when they're stuck in their own stories of victimhood, which means that they can end up just focusing on today (in the hope that by tomorrow, some miracle will have magically manifested itself). For magic to happen, it needs a helping hand - which either needs to come from a partner or spouse (who can help the Prisoner build their confidence by working **with** them to expand their comfort zones) or someone who can provide professional advice.

How Prisoners handle money in relationships

When Prisoners are left to look after the money within the household, they'll do a good job - scrimping, saving, putting coins into separate jars to ensure that there's just enough. However, until they learn a better way of doing things, that's how things will remain, with there only being 'barely enough' to get by. Prisoners need to work with their partners to *plan* their way to a better future. First, the Prisoner needs to let go of their 'story' - for however tough things were in the past, history doesn't have to repeat itself and become the future. For Prisoners to get this, they need to be able to trust - and they'll need evidence. And lots of it. They'll be inspired by stories of others who've been in similar circumstances but who've broken free. Give them books, watch films with them - help the Prisoner see that they too, have what it takes to build a different, better future.

PRISONER: AS A PARENT

Prisoners take parenting seriously. They set the rules for the family and expect their children to abide by them. Often quite strict, they can be fair - although if they're in a bad place themselves, they might take their misery out on their children. Prisoner parents either 'do without' to make sure their children have everything they need (even if not everything they want) or they've given up completely and their offspring pretty much have to fend for themselves. Very unlucky children will have parents who are so stuck in their Shadow Prisoner that they've turned to the bottle, drugs - or both (and more besides). Prisoner parents can sometimes pin their's - and their children's - hopes on luck rather than effort.

Worth considering: Because of their own issues around money, Prisoner parents can end up holding onto the purse strings very tightly - and chide their children with well-worn comments like 'money doesn't grow on trees'. While children do of course, need to know the value of money, their Prisoner parents may unwittingly be teaching them that money is always going to be a 'struggle'. Inadvertently, they may be setting up repeating patterns of difficulty and unhappiness for ***their children's futures***.

PRISONER: AS A CHILD

Prisoner children are often sensible and 'older than their years'. This may be because they've had to be caretakers for their parents or families at some level (usually emotional and sometimes physical). Many Prisoner children have Prisoner parents - and the former learn from a very young age to see everything in life as a struggle.

They learn that they can get sympathy and attention through their tales of woe, which left unchecked can lead them to living a life filled with excuses. Prisoner children who succeed later in life can feel guilty that they've done 'better than their parents' - and may seek to assuage that guilt by buying their parents expensive gifts like houses or cars, if and when they can afford it.

Worth considering: Prisoner children should be encouraged to step into their own power and challenged to expand their comfort zones. When it comes to finances, Prisoner children need to learn how to make money for themselves. As well as doing odd jobs for pocket money - which increases their belief in themselves, Prisoner children also lap up 'hero's quest' type stories in which hard work wins the day!

PRISONER: HOW THEY RELATE TO TIME

Poverty in one area of life often spills over into other areas too. In this case, the Prisoner's shortage of money often goes hand in hand with a shortage of time. Either they're having to do more than one job to make ends meet, or they're having to run around town comparing prices to make their food budgets go further. Proud Prisoners value punctuality and see it as a mark of respect, while those who are bitter and resentful sometimes behave passive aggressively and turn up late in a subconscious bid to 'get even' with people who they envy.

How the Prisoner breaches boundaries around time

Prisoners can waste time by focusing on everything that they don't want - rather than planning how to get to where they want to be.

PRISONER: WHAT THEY WEAR

Maybe it won't come as that much of a surprise but Prisoners don't particularly dress to impress - sometimes it's because they just can't afford to, often it's because their clothes reflect their damaged self-esteem.

Unfortunately, while none of us should 'judge a book by its cover', research does show that whether we like it or not, first impressions do count. When the Prisoner looks down at heel, they give off a negative vibe, which subconsciously affects how others perceive them. But when they make an effort to look their best, they feel good too, which in turn builds their self-confidence. How much something costs isn't important - wearing clothes that fit properly and suit us is.

HOW OTHER - HIGH SCORING - 'MONEY TYPES' CAN INFLUENCE THE PRISONER

Prisoner - Pharaoh:

This individual leads from the front - and they're driven to fight to the end for those causes in which they passionately believe. They're able to rally and lead the fight against the wrongs of this world. Fuelled by a heady mixture of injustice and determination, their ability to rally the troops can be legendary.

However, while all of the above is certainly true for the enlightened Prisoner-Pharaoh, more commonly there's a tendency for them to express haughty displeasure and self-pity at the unfair hand life has dealt them. They often believe that they deserve *more* (preferably without having to work for it) just because, well, they say so!

Watch out for: Fighting doggedly for what seems like a 'worthy cause' can lead to others perceiving the Prisoner-Pharaoh as obsessive, angry or judgemental. Worse, their innate sense of 'entitlement' can leave those around them feeling exhausted. The result? The Prisoner-Pharaoh can end up feeling rejected and alone, which deepens their anger and resentment at the world.

Moving forwards: The Prisoner-Pharaoh needs to drop their unhealthy sense of entitlement and replace it with a positive attitude from which purposeful work and collaboration can yield healthy and satisfying results. They'd also do well to remember that people are more inclined to want to fight *for* - rather than *against* - something.

Prisoner - Magician:

This individual is able to see what *isn't* working and what most definitely needs to be fixed. Able to bring entrepreneurial vision to the projects with which they get involved, they *create solutions* rather than just complain about things not being right. And if they're feeling positive, they're also able to see how a project can be monetised - a key component for many worthwhile endeavours.

Watch out for: The Prisoner-Magician needs to guard against 'talking a good talk' while failing to *take action*.

Moving forwards: While this individual can benefit from acknowledging the mistakes of the past, they do well to focus on the solutions that can be created *now*.

Prisoner - Joker:

With their ability to connect and engage, this individual recognises that all great projects are achieved through *people*. They're easily able to attract people to fight alongside them and they ensure their gang is *the* cool place to hang out. They inherently know how to be diplomatic, which means that they can, on occasion, simply use the power of persuasion to seize the day.

Watch out for: The Prisoner-Joker needs to ensure that they don't end up fighting for the sake of it. They need to learn to leave their egos behind and instead to follow the wisdom of their hearts to ensure that what they're seeking to change is actually in *everyone's* best interests, and not just their own. Equally, they need to guard against just 'bunking off', as they're not always aware that some consistently applied effort can often yield some tantalisingly exciting results.

Moving forwards: The Prisoner-Joker needs to remember that humour and generosity of spirit go a long way - and that winning their 'enemies' over is far easier (and less expensive) than fighting them.

Prisoner - Angel:

This individual displays the compassionate and intuitive nature of the Angel - which means that however tough the Prisoner has it, they still want to help those they perceive as worse off than themselves. This characteristic can win the Prisoner-Angel approval from others, but they need to ensure that the positive strokes that they happily receive aren't, inadvertently, keeping them stuck.

Watch out for: The Prisoner-Angel often focuses on others to their own detriment - leaving themselves out, which ultimately leads to resentment and fatigue. Used wisely, the Angel aspect can help shine a light on what's not working for the Prisoner - inviting this individual to explore **inwards**, rather than remaining trapped behind the bars of their own making.

Moving forwards: The Prisoner-Angel needs to understand that establishing boundaries and looking after themselves **first** is the most selfless thing they can do. When they 'own' what isn't working and seek out people who have overcome similar adversities, they're able to rise to the challenge and follow in their hero's or heroine's footsteps.

Prisoner - Architect:

In order not to repeat the patterns of the past, this individual does well to use its Architect's talents for working out what went wrong - and working out a plan for doing things differently next time. They also benefit from recalling the famous words of Albert Einstein who said, "We cannot solve our problems with the same thinking we used when we created them."

Watch out for: The Prisoner-Architect needs to guard against incessantly whinging about every small detail of what's not working for them. Boring or irritating everyone around them isn't the best way to win friends and influence people.

Moving forwards: By choosing a relatively small goal to start with, the Prisoner-Architect can strengthen their practical resolve by chunking things down into manageable pieces so that they can take **daily** small steps to move things along. Achieving - and celebrating - a successful outcome in this way encourages them to repeat the process with more challenging objectives.

SECTION 2

COACHING STORIES STRAIGHT FROM THE COUCH
How the 'Money Types' offer simple solutions to
solve often complex problems

WITH MORE THAN ENOUGH IN THE BANK, JIM AND PAM WERE STILL ARGUING ABOUT MONEY...

Jim and Pam glared at each other. Each felt that they were right - and that the other was wrong. They both turned and looked at me, seemingly the referee.

This was a second marriage for them both. Jim had never wanted children - although by his own admission, he was enjoying being a step-father to Pam's grown up daughter and son.

In their day-to-day lives, Jim and Pam got on really well. Both had a love of travelling, eating out and going to the theatre. They were also enjoying having their newly-built house decorated to suit their taste. However, underlying their relationship was a simmering disagreement about money. Jim was proud of his business achievements and even though he'd never have boasted to anyone else, much of his confidence came from having a large investment portfolio. Like many people with a high 'Pharaoh' score, Jim's self-worth was wrapped up in his net-worth.

Pam however, was struggling with what she perceived as Jim's meanness. She was becoming increasingly hurt and frustrated at his refusal to use a little of their joint money to help out her children with a house deposit.

Digging her fingernails into the palms of her hands, she looked at Jim and muttered, "We have more than enough for everything we could possibly need. I just don't see why we can't give them some money now - when they could really do with it."

Jim's by-now oft-repeated reply was that he'd had to work hard for everything in life with no handouts - and he didn't see why her children couldn't do the same. He also pointed out that in the long run, the children would be robbed of the satisfaction that comes from hard work if money were simply handed to them on a plate.

Jim and Pam were at an impasse.

The first step to helping them break free was enabling them both to understand that neither was being difficult for the sake of it. Rather, it was a case of their respective 'Money Types' playing out differently.

As a 'Pharaoh', Jim's self-regard came not only from how much he was worth financially, but also by being held in high esteem as a leader. While he wasn't aware of it consciously, his sub-conscious fear was that if he gave money to the children now, he'd somehow lose their respect - because on paper, he'd be worth less.

Recognising the truth of this - which until now had been hidden in his 'shadow' - enabled Jim to shift his perspective.

Equally, Pam's Shadow 'Angel' had been playing out unwittingly too. As well as wanting to help her children out, there'd also been a hidden part of her that felt that giving them a house deposit would encourage them to visit more often - out of gratitude.

What Jim and Pam both had in common was that they'd not wanted to lose the love, respect and connection they had with the children - or with each other.

With this new clarity - and commitment to respecting each other's needs - they were able to work out a plan of action that created a win:win not only for Jim and Pam but also for the rest of the family.

DENNIS DISCOVERS THAT WHAT CAN SEEM EXPENSIVE CAN BE THE BEST VALUE...

Just fifteen minutes before my personal development workshop was set to start, I noticed one of the participants sitting on his own, glowering over his cup of coffee with beads of angry sweat dripping down his temple.

Somewhat perturbed, I thought I'd better find out what was wrong - acutely aware that his negativity was likely to infect everyone in the room if I didn't deal with it swiftly.

Before I even managed to open my mouth, Dennis turned to me and asked in an angry tone how he was ever supposed to be happy when his ex-wife had been 'taking him for alimony' for years.

"Worse, she spends the money on such ridiculously frivolous things. Last month, she even used the money to pay for a white parrot! I think she's just doing it to wind me up."

I'll admit that the bit about the parrot wasn't quite what I'd been expecting - and it was all I could do to suppress the urge to laugh. (Well, I do have quite a lot of the Joker 'Money Type' myself.)

I also wondered just how expensive a parrot could be?

I asked him how much maintenance he was paying and he assured me his anger wasn't about the money, but about the 'principle'. (That's the Shadow Pharaoh coming out to play).

I pressed him again, and he admitted that he'd been paying his ex-wife £65 a month for a considerable number of years. Both he and his new wife were resentful.

"Are you happy with your new wife?", I asked.

"Yes, I love my wife - and I love my life now!", he replied.

After a small pause, I said, "Actually, isn't £65 a month a really **tiny price** to pay for a happy life, with the woman you love by your side?"

There was another pause, although no proverbial pin dropped. He suddenly stood up, his previously angry face breaking out into a big grin. "You know, that one question has just answered everything for me. Thank you. I don't even need to attend the rest of your workshop now!"

And with that, he gave me a quick hug - and left.

ANTHEA LEARNS THAT STRUCTURE ENSURES YOU GET TO LIVE A FUN-FILLED LIFE...

Anthea was a fun client who was determined to drink every last drop that life could possibly offer - however, as she was getting older she began to see that unless things changed, she was going to run out of money before she ran out of life...

Very clearly a Joker 'Money Type', Anthea had grinned broadly when I'd pointed out that spending in the moment came very easily to her. Indeed, her strong Joker had happily been ruling the roost for most of her life - which had certainly been fun, varied and exciting.

Anthea also had a high Angel score - and while she was keen to get the most out of life herself, she was also very happy to share what she had with others. She'd taken the approach that 'what goes around, comes around' but while her friendship circle had grown, her bank accounts certainly hadn't.

It was time to introduce Anthea to her Architect.

I gently pointed out that 'peace of mind' and a 'financially secure future' required the wisdom that only her Architect could provide.

Anthea had groaned and grimaced - admitting that she'd previously dismissed any idea of structure, planning and routine as being boring.

A little later in the conversation, Anthea had gone on to admit that while she'd inherited a generous sum when she was younger, she'd been burned on more than one occasion by people 'using her' for her money.

And it wasn't just people close to her emotionally who'd taken advantage, she'd also been 'played' by a couple of businessmen who'd been keen to tap into her financial reserves to underwrite their supposedly 'can't fail' entrepreneurial ideas. They'd offered her a generous return on her investment - but when things hadn't quite gone to plan, they'd had no qualms about shutting everything down and simply walking away. It was Anthea who'd borne the losses.

Understandably, she was keen to stop it happening again.

"Maybe," I'd suggested, "this is where we could bring your Architect into play. Rather than just accepting invitations or supposed business opportunities on the spur of the moment (a Shadow Joker response), you could use your Architect to **set boundaries** for you.

"You might even find it helpful to use Architect language to buy you time. For example, you could respond to any future invitations to join a big 'deal' with: 'This sounds really interesting. However, it's **my policy** to give myself time to consider a new project **before** I'll even think about a more detailed discussion. Let me have a think about it and I'll get back to you next week…'.

I explained, "This will enable you to buy yourself time to undertake some 'due diligence'. As well as doing some background checking, you can also use the time to consider what problems could arise and what questions you **should** be asking. And it'll give you a chance to think about why - and whether - this is a project you really do want to get involved in at all."

By distancing herself in this way from the initial enthusiasm and excitement of the Joker, Anthea would be able to draw on the wisdom and experience of the Architect - whose strength is 'in the detail' and checking the 'fine print'.

As our time together concluded, Anthea looked relieved. With her Architect in place, she already felt more confident that she wouldn't allow what remained of her inheritance to slip through her fingers.

She also agreed to seek independent investment advice. Her Architect immediately recognised that by finding out how to invest her money wisely (and prudently), she'd be able to enjoy a more comfortable old age.

TERRY FINALLY WORKS OUT THE CAUSE OF HIS FRUSTRATING EXAM FAILURES...

As a child, Terry had been deeply angry with his father who'd treated his mother appallingly. Perhaps unsurprisingly, he'd grown up feeling trapped and helpless. Very much living in the shadow side of the Prisoner, Terry had relied on passive aggressive behaviour to survive.

Sitting in my office, Terry had nonchalantly shrugged his shoulders - saying that it didn't matter, 'his father would pay'. As I'd looked back at him silently, it'd been all I could do to mask my distaste for his entitled Shadow Pharaoh attitude.

Here was a 26-year-old young man telling me his woeful story about yet again failing his professional accountancy exams but rather than being worried, Terry had instead been sporting a disdainful look. For some reason or other, he'd come to the conclusion that the whole world owed him a living.

Terry was a hard man to like and the tone and arrogance of his conversation hadn't really helped. Terry's father had not only made – and paid for - an appointment for his son with me but he'd also been picking up the tab for all of his son's tuition, re-sit **and** living expenses.

Refusing to get a job on the pretext that he needed to study all day, Terry had been quite happy to use his father's hard-earned money to finance not only his studies but also his expensive social life.

Clearly, he'd been onto a good number. His father had wanted Terry to see me because he'd recognised that his son had a block when it came to passing exams – and he'd thought that I'd be able to help.

While Terry's behaviour appeared to be completely selfish, I knew that something must have happened earlier in his life to make him that way.

But before we went into a deeper discussion, I'd first asked Terry why he wanted to become an accountant.

His response had been chilling. While he'd admitted that he'd always liked maths, he didn't have any real desire whatsoever to be an accountant. More interested in easy money than anything else, Terry had believed that accountancy would at least earn him some status, as well as guarantee him an income.

He'd winced when I'd gently suggested that he didn't really need a job for a steady income, as by repeatedly failing all his exams, Terry could seemingly simply rely on his father to provide him with money - without his having to go out to work at all!

With this perhaps harsh - but fresh - perspective, the penny had begun to slowly drop.

Failing his exams, I'd explained, was a 'symptom' rather than the cause. Finally recognising that perhaps he needed to start taking responsibility for his own life, Terry had agreed to try hypnosis with me in order to discover what was at the root of the problem.

Once he was in a state of complete relaxation, I'd asked Terry why he was punishing his father. At first he hadn't answered but soon the tears had started rolling as the whole story came tumbling out.

As a teenager his father had enjoyed several extra-marital affairs, which had ultimately resulted in his parents' divorce. His mother had suffered a mental breakdown. Terry had blamed his father totally.

Intuitively, I knew there was more to come. Taking him back still further, Terry had gasped in horror as one of his earliest memories came flooding back. As a child, he'd remembered being unable to sleep and when he had gone downstairs he'd found his parents violently, but somehow silently, rowing.

His father had then started hitting his wife and the young Terry had fled back to his bedroom in fear and anger, ***vowing that he would get even with his father when he grew up***.

While still in a state of hypnosis, I'd gently asked Terry to imagine his father was in the room with us today – and I'd invited him to have the conversation that he'd needed to have had as a child. I softly guided him to first express his anger and then, when he was ready, to make the decision to forgive his father. As I'd explained, it wasn't about condoning his father's actions - but it was necessary if he were to release himself from the painful ties of the past.

Finally, still within the light state of trance, I'd invited Terry to step into his Pharaoh personal power and to make a commitment to his father that he, Terry, was going to take charge of his own life now and stop punishing his father by playing the Shadow Prisoner victim and failing his exams.

Afterwards, when he'd come back to waking reality, Terry had looked like a completely different young man. Wiping the last of the tears from his eyes, he'd smiled and taken out his own cheque-book to pay for the session saying, "From now on, the buck stops with me!"

SARAH FINALLY UNLOCKS HER TROUBLESOME BLINDSPOT WHEN IT COMES TO MONEY...

Settling down to her cup of coffee, Sarah casually mentioned that she knew she was useless with money, freely admitting that she "just can't understand the numbers".

Having used that same excuse myself a long while back, I wasn't sure if I totally believed her - especially when I'd watched her easily totting up the number of days' holiday she'd already taken (and how many she had left) and what flexitime she was owed by her employer.

As a tiny experiment, I casually wrote down the same list of numbers that she'd previously been calculating and put a pound sign in front of them all - and invited her simply to add the list up again.

This time, blind panic crossed her face and her brow furrowed.

The numbers were exactly the same - it was the pound sign that was triggering her anxiety.

The anxiety probably arose from the memory of a few financial problems she'd had in the past - when a combination of her overly-generous Shadow Angel and stuck-victim Shadow Prisoner had left her with seemingly unmanageable debts. Perhaps unsurprisingly, her mind had created a powerful but negative link between 'money' and 'numbers'.

The result? Panic.

When we panic, not only does our creativity switch off - but we also often become unable to see what's right in front of us. (If you've ever tried looking for something important when you're running late for an appointment, only to have it turn up later exactly where you left it, you'll know exactly what I'm talking about.)

Worse, we start **making up a story** around what's happening - and it's not long before we're incorrectly linking cause and effect. Inadvertently, we end up casting a negative spell on ourselves.

How could Sarah break the spell?

First she needed to become aware of what was going on - and then she needed to choose a different, more helpful story. She decided to say to herself: "I'd always thought I was bad with numbers - but then someone showed me that this simply wasn't true. IF I'm actually better with numbers than I thought - well, maybe I'm better with money than I thought, too."

If we're going to tell ourselves stories (and we all do), then rather than tell ourselves negative ones that focus on our fears, let's instead choose to create positive stories for ourselves that focus on helping us get the results we want.

Oh - and of course, this doesn't all only apply to money...

STEVE CALLS ON HIS MAGICIAN TO STEP UP INTO THE CAREER HE TRULY WANTED...

Steve had been devastated when he'd received the news that he was being made redundant. He'd always worked hard for his company and had diligently made sure that - with his high Architect - he'd delivered everything his bosses had asked for, on time and within budget.

He'd come to be sitting in my office on the recommendation of his lawyer - who'd recognised that Steve would need help coming to terms with the sudden changes in his circumstances.

Angry - and somewhat passive aggressive - Steve had folded his arms and asked me what I was going to do to help him find another job.

Of course, getting another job was actually down to Steve himself - my role was to find a way to turn this rude interruption in his career into a gift. If we could turn this tough situation into an opportunity for Steve to progress his career (and maybe bank some of his redundancy payment) then I'd be delighted on his behalf.

At first, it was proving hard to get Steve to articulate what direction he wanted his career to go in. He ruefully confessed that he'd completely lost his mojo. While he'd put together a comprehensive CV, it was a dull, dry list of all the jobs he'd held held in the past.

After more discussion, he admitted that more than anything, he wanted to be in a senior position where he was in his own words, 'Seen as a decision maker'.

Something clicked. I could see what was going on. It was his Shadow Pharaoh that was desperate for recognition and that wanted to be acknowledged. His focus was on himself...rather than on what his skills and talents ***could bring to a prospective company***.

With his high Architect score, Steve had been relying on doing only what was asked of him by his previous employers - and this was reflected in his CV. His Architect was doing all it could to keep him safe - but the prospect of remaining in his tried-but-tested comfort zone was leaving him feeling bored and 'grey'.

What he needed to do now was to transcend his focus away from just himself...to both himself and his future employer.

In order for him to step up, he needed to introduce the wisdom of his Magician.

I pointed out to Steve that very often, people running businesses have a high Magician. "They're the ones who have a visionary approach, who spot opportunities and who shape their organisations to maximise profits by innovating and bringing new things to market.

"And they keep abreast of what's going on - not just within their own industry, but in others too, so that they can benefit from cross-pollinating ideas. They're life-long learners and they get to those higher positions by not just doing the 'job' but also by **being** who they are and bringing their full selves to the party.

"They don't apply for jobs saying that they want to be 'decision makers'. Why not? Because it's a given that they already **are** decision makers. That's the level they work at...it's how they already know themselves and it's how others perceive them too."

I finished by suggesting that maybe he could use the time he'd been inadvertently gifted by doing what high level Magicians do - which is to immerse themselves in piles of reading about their industry, the economy and future trends.

Indeed, rather like the old adage of 'dressing for the job you want, not the one you're in', it was time for Steve to start **behaving** like the people in whose footsteps he wanted to follow.

Steve suddenly smiled. The penny had dropped. It was as though a weight had lifted not only from his shoulders, but also from his heart. Laughing, he agreed that maybe this period of rest between jobs was an unexpected opportunity after all.

The good news? It wasn't long before Steve sent me a happy text saying that he'd been introduced to an exciting new venture-capital-funded start-up company - and that he'd been ***invited to join the team at board level and he'd be earning a higher salary too!***

PETER AND ALAIA CHANGE THEIR APPROACH TO MONEY AND HAVE A HAPPIER MARRIAGE...

When Peter and Alaia met, there was an instant attraction - and nobody had been surprised when they'd married just nine months later. But a year into their marriage, small spats were rapidly growing into bigger temper tantrums.

While they both clearly loved each other and had no regrets about marrying, each was saddened that there seemed to be a chasm they just couldn't bridge. Like their family and friends, they put their disagreements down to their considerable age gap and different cultural heritages.

They readily accepted my suggestion that we see what the 'Money Types' would have to say. Peter had a high score for both Pharaoh and Architect - while Alaia was a Magician, with pretty high scores too for Angel and Joker.

The cause of the friction soon became clear...

With his high Pharaoh score, feeling respected and heard was important for Peter. While he wasn't expecting his wife to be deferential, he did feel undermined when faced with her astonishing ability to think quickly on her feet. He loved her intelligence and her caring nature - but often, he found himself feeling diminished in a way that he just couldn't put his finger on.

In turn, Alaia couldn't understand why he seemingly dismissed all her ideas. And she was particularly incensed when he asked her to record all her expenditure on a monthly spreadsheet. That wasn't how she rolled at all!

Gaining clarity brings relief...

Peter quickly realised that his Pharaoh and Architect combination could come across as a bit intimidating - and as he harked back to the couple's early days, he movingly admitted that it was Alaia's vivacity and fun nature that had been so alluring. Quickly, he realised that he was in danger of quashing the very things he loved most about her!

In turn Alaia, a bit of a self-confessed shopaholic, came to see that Peter wasn't asking for her receipts because he didn't trust her - but because when he could see everything laid out before him in a spreadsheet, he felt a sense of **control** over their joint finances.

One key lesson for them both was to recognise that while Alaia's Magician was ace at spotting opportunities and solutions - it was Peter's Architect ability to work out the finer detail that would bring their plans to fruition.

Interestingly, as they began to understand what had been happening - and why, their body language started to shift. He touched her arm, she shifted closer to him.

Fast forward a couple of months, and I received a thank you card from Alaia, in which she said that their marriage had transformed immeasurably. In the card, she'd written, "We both understand and respect each other now in a way that we simply didn't before - and **we no longer argue about money!**"

DAVID LEARNS THE IMPORTANCE OF USING THE POWER OF HIS PHARAOH WISELY...

David was a popular businessman who was liked and trusted within the community. He came to be sitting in my office however, because he'd been getting irritable with a number of people - especially on the road.

While these episodes could hardly be described as full blown road rage, they were causing problems between David and his wife, and he wanted to put a stop to his irritation. He'd been putting it down to stress - but he was beginning to feel that perhaps there was more to it.

He had indeed been working hard for the previous couple of years and he'd been determined to reach a target turnover and profit number for his business. He was pretty much on track - but rather than ask people for help, he'd instead been trying to do it all himself. That strategy had been working to a point - but then over-tiredness was causing him to lose his temper.

Mindful of not wanting to be like his difficult father - who often had all his own employees cowering in fear - David had instead been masking his feelings. But as he got more tired, his Shadow Pharaoh had increasingly been revealing itself.

It wanted to demand (rather than ask nicely!) that everyone within earshot drop everything and do what he said, without question. He even admitted that there was a little part of him that wanted people to acknowledge his status as a leader and employer - and that he'd increasingly been feeling as though he were being taken for granted.

We discussed what had had been happening, and as is so often the case, using the 'Money Types' language simplified everything.

"Not wanting to throw your weight around like your father - who spent a lifetime being ruled by his own Shadow Pharaoh - has stopped you from being honest with those around you. Actually, it's stopped you from being able to speak up assertively. As a consequence, you bottle everything up - and when the pressure gets too great, you explode. This in turn will have left you feeling guilty - and determined not to allow it to happen again. But of course it will have done - and it will have become a vicious cycle."

David nodded. What I was saying definitely chimed with his experience.

I continued, "In its 'light' side, the Pharaoh is the wise ruler, who takes the needs of the individual, the team and the organisation into account. It focuses on 'what's right - and not who's right'.

"You know, I'd even go as far as to say that we're only fully able to step into our own 'sovereignty' - and speak assertively - when we truly choose to **own** our Pharaoh."

I went on to explain that I've seen countless clients who've been highly capable and who've run successful teams and businesses - but who have not yet claimed their own emotional 'sovereignty'. Why? Because they'd been on the receiving end of petulant, demanding and bullying Shadow Pharaoh behaviours themselves and they'd vowed never to behave like that with other people.

"It's really a case of throwing the baby out with the bath water. Learning to be in our power - to 'command' rather than 'demand' - and to ask for what we need assertively, but not aggressively, is the goal. If we choose to simply avoid potential conflict and just instead 'be nice to everyone', we keep ourselves small. This leads to resentment building up and it inevitably spills out in the office, at home or on the road - as you've already experienced."

I finished by pointing out that we all need our Pharaoh to be strong - as it holds the vision for what we're truly here to accomplish in our lives. Given its rightful place, the Pharaoh also leads the rest of our personal 'Money Types' tribe too - giving them direction and purpose.

Armed with an understanding of why he'd been behaving the way he had brought instant relief to David. He also admitted that changing his behaviours wouldn't be easy - but knowing that the invitation was to allow his Pharaoh to take its rightful place was a great place to start.

MELISSA DISCOVERS WHY SHE KEEPS PLAYING OUT THE SAME COSTLY PATTERN...

Full of ideas - and energy - Melissa had been running her own marketing company for several years. While she'd had a moderate amount of success, she certainly wasn't where she'd expected to be after all her hard graft.

With her high Joker, she was a fun person with loads of enthusiasm and it was easy to see why her clients loved her. And as she spoke about the work she did on their behalf, it was clear that she really knew her stuff.

She'd even got to the point where she'd taken on a few members of staff - but while turnover had increased, Melissa's personal bank balance seemed to remain resolutely static. She admitted with an embarrassed giggle that she often worried that her personal finances were close to collapse.

Unsure of why she was so stuck, she'd decided to book a session with me.

After some discussion, it became clear that Melissa was good at winning new clients - and that they were happy to pay for the work her company was doing on their behalf. Her fees were reasonable, she was retaining clients and she had always made sure that her accounts were kept up to date.

We agreed - it wasn't her business that was a problem. It was more a case of her business reflecting a problem that lay *within her*.

I'd gone on to mention that the idea of the mind-body connection (in which the body plays out what is going on within the mind) is now becoming increasingly well accepted. I gently suggested that it wasn't such a big stretch to consider that our 'business' could in a way, perform the same function as our 'body' in terms of reflecting what is going on within the people running it. Indeed, the root of the word 'corporate' comes from the Latin 'corpus' - which means 'body'.

Melissa had smiled at this thought and together, we'd made a start on investigating her subconscious thoughts and beliefs - beginning with money and then widening the search.

Melissa had always relied on her Magician throughout her life, not just in business. She thrived on spotting opportunities and solving problems. Laughingly, she'd told me that she'd built a reputation on her ability to avert a last minute crisis by being able to 'pull the white rabbit out of the hat' in the nick of time.

My mind did a double take. This was familiar territory for me too.

Earlier in my own career, my ability to pull the 'white rabbit out of the hat' at the last minute was something I'd initially prided myself on - but I'd later gone on to recognise that it was actually a compulsion, if not an addiction. I'd enjoyed the sense of accomplishing something useful and being the kind of person that the team really needed - but when I'd eventually twigged what was going on I'd been forced to see that actually, I'd been subconsciously generating problems *in order to be* the Magician heroine who could 'sort things out'!

Through my Shadow Magician, my ego had been beautifully enabling my identity as a 'problem solver' to thrive - but the reality was that I'd been stuck in a loop and going around in circles - rather than making any real forward progress.

It had been another 'clever' form of being a busy fool.

As I'd shared my own experiences with Melissa, she'd instantly recognised that she'd been playing the same game too.

With knowledge, comes power.

While she now understood what had been going on, Melissa was worried that she might unwittingly still fall back into bad habits.

I quickly reassured her. Now that we'd identified the cause of her problem we could proceed to the second step, which was for her to re-identify and articulate her bigger goals and to use her very capable Magician to turn them into reality. With more exciting goals in place, she could keep her Magician happy by using its wisdom to make forward progress, rather than going around in circles.

At the same time, Melissa would need to consciously monitor herself for the next couple of months to question every action she was about to undertake. Was what she was about to do going to move her ***towards*** accomplishing her bigger goals or was it simply following her old pattern of creating and chasing distractions?

The final step was for Melissa to bring her Architect into play - which would encourage her to plan, organise and communicate clearly to her team. Developing her Architect would enable her to implement proven systems and processes into her business - so that there simply wouldn't be any last minute problems (or at least there'd be fewer) cropping up for her to leap in to solve.

The result?

Melissa reported on progress six months later. She happily admitted to feeling mentally freer with fewer distractions. And the really encouraging news was that her personal bank balance was now rapidly improving each month.

STEPHEN FOCUSES ON DOING WHAT IT TAKES TO EARN THE FABULOUS CAR OF HIS DREAMS...

Stephen had first visited my office three years ago. Then he'd complained of being bored at work and overweight. We'd discussed his lack of goals and ambition – and the detrimental effect this was having on his well-being.

Together we'd explored Stephen's aspirations – together with his childhood dreams. We'd agreed that not all goals needed to be financial ones – but as he had a fairly happy home life, Stephen had wanted to set himself a challenging goal that would give him a sense of real purpose at *work*.

As we'd chatted, Stephen had recalled that as a boy, he'd been an enormous fan of James Bond - and he'd boasted that one day he would own an Aston Martin like his childhood hero.

However, as an adult, everyday life had soon overshadowed his dreams and Stephen had become bogged down with earning enough money to pay the bills and keep a roof over his head.

Worse, Stephen's self-belief had been severely knocked as a child when his father had laughed at his dreams of owning such a beautiful car. Patting Stephen on the head, his father had told him to remember his station in life saying, "Everyone in our family has always had to work hard just to survive – don't you expect to be any different."

Like so many children before him, Stephen had unwittingly - and inadvertently - been indoctrinated with his parents Prisoner victim beliefs. His father's phrase about 'knowing one's station in life' was tantamount to saying that nothing could be changed and that 'one should just accept one's lot'.

In order for Stephen to succeed with his new goal, it was obvious that he was going to have to re-programme his sub-conscious mind at a deep level. Firstly, he would need to delete his father's negative thought patterns. In order to do that, Stephen would need to see that even if his advice had been misguided and unhelpful, his father had only been trying to protect him.

Secondly, Stephen needed to forgive his father – whose beliefs he could now see had held him back in many areas for most of his life. By forgiving his father, Stephen was not condoning his actions, but was merely untying himself from the negative energy that had been weighing him down.

After using our session - in which I'd used guided visualisation - to help him let go of his father's thought patterns, Stephen was now free to focus on his future goal.

Looking more enthused than he had for a while, Stephen set himself a SMART goal of buying a new silver Aston Martin - within just three years. As well as the streamlined beauty of the vehicle itself, Stephen had chosen the Aston Martin because of the James Bond symbolism.

I'd shown Stephen how to visualise living his goal as though it were his new reality – and he'd promised to spend ten minutes each day imagining what it would feel like to drive the car of his dreams. I'd also encouraged him to spend some time thinking about how he'd look *in* the car - along with what the view would be like from ***behind*** the wheel.

Of course, imagining making his dreams come true was only the first step. Stephen and I had also spent an intense hour or so debating, discussing and creating an action plan that would enable him to earn the additional money he needed to turn his dream into a reality.

Next we invited Stephen's Magician into the picture - after all, it's the Magician which is able to spot opportunities and Stephen was definitely going to need to draw on its wisdom if he was going to succeed with his ambitious goal.

He admitted that he'd been playing with a business idea in his mind for some time - but that he'd dismissed it as being too far outside of his 'day job'. But he also recognised that if he were to make more money - much more money - than ever before, then he'd need to start doing things differently.

Acknowledging that he was unafraid of hard work, Stephen excitedly started scribbling some figures down and he knew that if he were prepared to put the hours in to bring his new venture to life, he could soon be on track to buy the Aston Martin model on which his heart was truly set.

While Stephen may have had a mere pipe-dream before, the difference now was that he had massive self-belief. He'd stepped into his own Pharaoh sovereignty and he'd programmed his mind to ***believe*** that he could succeed.

Fast forward to three years later - and Stephen was once more in my office. But this time, I was standing opposite an enthusiastic, vibrant and excited individual. Stephen proudly told me that he'd dropped into my office in the hope that he could take me out to lunch – in his shiny new silver Aston Martin DB9!

SECTION 3

DISCOVER THE NINE MONEY STORIES
THAT KEEP PEOPLE TRAPPED
...and find out how the 'Money Types'
can help you break free!

While a few people naturally have a comfortable relationship with Money, the majority do not. And intriguingly, our relationship with money has less to do with how much is in our bank accounts - and much, much more to do with our subconscious **beliefs** about money.

Of course, many of these beliefs were created in childhood - and knowing no differently, we simply assimilated them as 'truth'.

The result?

When it comes to money, our vision is skewed. Whether we believe that the 'love of money is the root of all evil' or that 'money doesn't grow on trees' - or we've had to watch those looking after us scrabble down the back of the sofa to find a few odd coins to buy that night's dinner, we come to blame 'Money'. After all, isn't it 'Money' that's causing all the angst?

But it isn't. It can't be. Money is a neutral force. An 'energy', if you will. It's what we **project onto** Money that's the problem - because money is simply a mirror, reflecting back to us our own deeply buried fears. Fears of not being good enough, of not deserving, of not being worthy. We're taught not to be greedy. And yet, the **more** we have, the **more** we can do with it. (But it's down to us - and our core values - to decide whether we'll use our financial reserves wisely or selfishly.)

Money is a paradox, but all too often, we only get to see one facet - the facet we **fear**. But when we lean into it, rather than bury our head in the sand or shrug our shoulders with a 'nothing I can do about it' attitude, a whole new world of possibility opens up.

What I've found in my work with organisations and teams is that success is only achieved when the **individuals** involved are in their 'sovereignty'. Indeed, "Successful companies employ successful individuals" is now my credo. And while there's a wealth of fabulous training available - from leadership and personal development through to selling and business development - our **personal relationship with 'Money'** very rarely gets a mention. But from my experience of coaching a variety of different people - from business leaders in the UK and the USA, to one-man-band operations in Brazil and New Zealand, one thing stands out: until we uncover the hidden stories we're running about 'Money', we never get to step into our full 'sovereignty'.

Having worked with thousands of individuals over the last couple of decades, I've now identified the 9 most common 'Money Stories' that hold people back. I've identified with several of them along the way myself - and I have a hunch that at least a couple might resonate with you too. As well as describing the stories below, I've also shared some helpful information about how each of the six 'Money Types' can help (or hinder) you on your journey.

The Nine Money Stories:

1 **"There's never enough - no matter how hard I work or how much I earn..."**

2 **"I hate my job - but I can't afford to walk away..."**

3 **"I'm not great at maths - so I'll never be good with money..."**

4 **"My partner takes care of all our financial stuff..."**

5 **"It's just too late to make any difference to my finances..."**

6 **"I'm so deep in debt - nothing I do will make any difference..."**

7 **"I love working for myself but my business drains all my cash and energy..."**

8 **"People tell me that even though I'm smart, I'm not reaching my full potential..."**

9 **"All my time, money & energy goes into looking after the people I care about..."**

1

"THERE'S NEVER ENOUGH - NO MATTER HOW HARD I WORK OR HOW MUCH I EARN…"

Common with both ambitious and generous types, this 'Money Story' tends to rear its head once we get past the first flush of excitement when it comes to earning money for ourselves. After all, those heady days of stretching money as far as it'll go seem like an adventure when we're just starting out - but it becomes disappointing, debilitating and well, downright depressing when that sense of **not having enough** never seems to change.

The patterns that create this story often stem from childhood, when we're most likely to first acquire a sense of 'lack'. Whether it's hearing our parents tell us that 'money doesn't grow on trees', or watching them struggle to make ends meet, our subconscious minds register **anxiety** around money. As it happens, our subconscious minds not only store the memory of every single thing that's ever happened to us, but they also store the memory of how we **felt** at the time too. Little wonder that money starts to become something in our minds that we believe is 'going to cause us trouble'. But that's not even the worst of it. Our subconscious minds want to keep us safe (security is far more important to the subconscious mind than our happiness) - and it works on the belief that creating situations that repeat previous experiences is the safest thing it can do because, well - we're still here and alive, aren't we? Keeping us **alive** is the primary driver of the subconscious, not whether we're happy or achieving our ambitions.

In order to break free, we need to learn to over-ride the subconscious mind's preference for focusing on the past - and we can do this by regularly focusing on the exciting vision of the **future** that we're looking to create for ourselves.

How your PHARAOH can help you: Make the decision that your past doesn't have to become your future - and put plans in place to take care of both 'today' and 'tomorrow'.

How your PHARAOH can hinder you: Arrogantly thinking it knows best and refusing to listen and learn from others.

How your MAGICIAN can help you: Focus on ONE 'side hustle' and build it so that it becomes a reliable 'cash cow'.

How your MAGICIAN can hinder you: Investing time, energy and money in every 'new idea' but never seeing any of these wonderful ideas through to completion.

How your JOKER can help you: Build relationships with successful people - after all, the company you keep is the best predictor of the kind of lifestyle you're destined to enjoy (or not!).

How your JOKER can hinder you: Living solely for today may be fun - but it's less fun when you're struggling to survive *tomorrow*.

How your ANGEL can help you: Learn to look after yourself first - that way, you prevent yourself becoming someone else's problem further down the line.

How your ANGEL can hinder you: Giving away everything you have to help those around you - which results in leaving yourself short.

How your ARCHITECT can help you: Plan for both today and the future - *saving* (even if only a little to begin with) builds new habits. And with every pay rise from now, choose to save more - that way, you'll begin to build a healthy pot for your future.

How your ARCHITECT can hinder you: Getting so bogged down with the detail that you never see - or enjoy - the bigger picture.

How your PRISONER can help you: See what isn't working and take the decision *today* to step into your power and make the necessary changes. Only *you* can do it!

How your PRISONER can hinder you: Choosing to see yourself as a victim guarantees that history will keep on repeating itself.

2

"I HATE MY JOB - BUT I CAN'T AFFORD TO WALK AWAY…"

All too often, that inviting career path we couldn't wait to tread loses its shine somewhere along the journey. Either it didn't live up to expectations - or we find that we're just bored.

And without a sense of forward progression and new frontiers to explore, we can come to resent the job we're in - fearing that this is 'going to be as good as it gets' for the rest of our lives.

Couple this deep-seated sense of disappointment with some hefty financial commitments and it's no wonder that there are lots of unhappy people struggling to find any joyful meaning in their work life.

The situation can worsen too, if you're feeling the weight of other people's expectations on your shoulders - especially if your family made sacrifices to finance your studies in the early days.

Know that fearing what other people might say if you were to switch paths now will keep you locked in a self-imposed life of 'conformity'. Don't you deserve better?

In order to break free, it's important to work out a plan *first*. Keep your ideas to yourself (to avoid other people raining on your parade) until you're sure that you've thought through every eventuality. Work out how you'll manage all your current commitments financially - and remember to take into account any learning time you'll require and any up-front costs that your new venture may require too.

And when it's time to share your thoughts, feelings and ideas with those closest to you, be generous and allow them time to consider all that you're saying. After all, you've had plenty of time to reach your decision - they haven't! Allow the positive people (the ones who want the best for you) to share the journey with you - you and they will both be happier for it.

How your PHARAOH can help you: Recognise that you're the leader of your own domain - and that the person who's opinion matters most is your own. This doesn't mean falling down on your commitments - plan carefully for how you can transition from where you are now to where you want to be.

How your PHARAOH can hinder: Believing that you will lose face if you admit that you're not happy with the work you're doing.

How your MAGICIAN can help you: Identify the work that brings you a sense of purpose and work out how you can leverage your ideas to provide so much value for others that they'll be queuing up to pay you. Figure out how you're going to implement the plan - and decide on **when** you're going to take action...and **do it**.

How your MAGICIAN can hinder you: Coming up with wonderful plans and exciting scenarios for how you **could** make the world a better place uses up so much energy that you never get round to actually **doing it**.

How your JOKER can help you: Network with people who can put you in contact with the kind of companies you'd love to work with - and which have a **need** for your particular gifts and talents.

How your JOKER can hinder you: Buying things to make yourself feel better to compensate for a job you don't like just increases your expenses - with the result that escaping your job will be all the harder because of your higher outgoings.

How your ANGEL can help you: Learn to put yourself, your needs and your desires first - after all, you're the one in charge of your own life. (And yes, getting to do work that you love should be your priority - after all you spend too many hours at work to put up with a job that perpetually makes you unhappy.)

How your ANGEL can hinder you: Working hard in a job you hate just to keep the money coming in for everyone else will result in you becoming ill, sooner or later.

How your ARCHITECT can help you: Research the kind of role you'd like to move into - and plan your escape. What additional education do you require? What skills do you need to develop? Set yourself a goal...and go for it.

How your ARCHITECT can hinder you: Convincing yourself that your spreadsheet shows that you can't afford to do things any differently.

How your PRISONER can help you: Use your imagination to see how things could be in the future - first look at how you'll feel if you stay where you are now and then tune into how you'd feel if you followed a more exciting career path. Come back into the present and decide which option you're going to take - and then plan for how you can make the magic happen.

How your PRISONER can hinder you: Negative chit chat around the water cooler feels cosy - and it's often more comfortable to moan with your work mates than to do something about it.

3 "I'M NOT GREAT AT MATHS - SO I'LL NEVER BE GOOD WITH MONEY..."

It's all too easy to confuse mathematical genius with ease around money - but there are plenty of people out there who are a 'duff' with numbers but who still have the Midas touch when it comes to filling their bank accounts.

Understanding money - how it works, how it grows and how you can use it to finance the lifestyle of your dreams is very different from sitting in tedious maths lessons at school, wondering how you'd ever apply what you were being taught.

Frighteningly, it's also all too easy to feel shame around not being a maths wizard - and to decide that if you're not good with numbers, then maybe you're not good at lots of other important stuff too. With this thought pattern, it's not long before you're projecting your negative beliefs onto your ability to handle money - and you end up turning what wasn't-even-true into your reality.

A bad situation becomes worse when we take other people's comments - and particularly their 'mocking' comments into consideration. But maybe it's now time to ask yourself why those people felt the need to put you down? People who are confident and happy in who they are **lift others up**, so have they been using your discomfort to make themselves feel better at your expense? (OK, let's be kind, maybe they didn't even know that they were doing it!)

In order to break free, simply recognise the truth - you can easily make money, even if numbers aren't your 'thing'. (And the really good news is that you can **hire** people who enjoy 'numbers' - leaving you free to do what you do best.)

How your PHARAOH can help you: Know that the most successful people employ the services of the best people they know - and are proud to do so.

How your PHARAOH can hinder you: Being so ashamed of your lack of mathematical ability that you fail to ask for professional help when it comes to managing your money.

How your MAGICIAN can help you: Use your ability to look at new projects from multiple perspectives and consider where you could lose - as well as make - money.

How your MAGICIAN can hinder you: Relying on 'guesstimates' can lead to costly confidence-knocking mistakes further down the line.

How your JOKER can help you: Check out your little black book of contacts to find out who can help you manage the money, so that you can focus on what you do best: building relationships.

How your JOKER can hinder you: Ignoring the 'boring numbers' can lead to higher-than-necessary expenses, reducing your profitability.

How your ANGEL can help you: Recognise that other people enjoy helping - just like you do - and when you ask for their help from the outset, it makes them feel good.

How your ANGEL can hinder you: Feeling that you're burdening someone else when you ask for help, you try your best to make sense of what just doesn't come easily to you - and you end up creating a mess of it all. (In the end you're forced to ask for help - and it's much harder for someone else to unpick what you've done than if they'd started the work from scratch. Feeling even more guilty leads to you repeating the same behaviour and thus an unhappy cycle worsens.)

How your ARCHITECT can help you: Create an efficient framework from the outset - and use it confidently to set targets and measure progress.

How your ARCHITECT can hinder you: Stressing, measuring and constantly tinkering away with the details can take up so much time that you fail to get out there in the market place, which leads to you earning less than you deserve.

How your PRISONER can help you: Break the link in your thinking and recognise that lots of people are good with money - despite not having excelled in maths at school. Decide to be one of them.

How your PRISONER can hinder: Fixating on what you're not good at simply keeps you stuck. Similarly, comparing your abilities with others never ends well.

"MY PARTNER TAKES CARE OF ALL OUR FINANCIAL STUFF..."

Often - but not always - this is a story that belongs more commonly to women, especially those who were brought up with parents who held 'traditional values'.

While it can feel easier - and is often tempting - to hand over financial control to a partner who at least on-the-face-of-it is 'comfortable with money', it does mean that effectively, you're giving your power away.

And it's often the people who've given their power away at the outset who find themselves facing tough and difficult lessons later on if their partner leaves, dies or even gambles it all away!

In order to break free, it's important to step up. Take an interest - talk with your partner about your desire to learn about money and see how they react. Usually, a partner will be relieved that they now get to share the responsibility for the financial wellbeing of your life together. However, on occasion, a partner might resent what they perceive to be a threat to their 'control'. This already tells you something - but either way, it's important to stick to your guns (even if it makes you feel really uncomfortable) after all, your financial future depends upon it.

How your PHARAOH can help you: Claim your sovereignty - and take an interest in what's going on financially in your relationship. Make sure you not only have your say but that you're also at the very least, kept informed.

How your PHARAOH can hinder you: Believing that you're too important - or too cherished - to have to look at the financial side of things can cost you dearly further down the line.

How your MAGICIAN can help you: Devise a strategy that'll take care of you both - even if the strategy is bringing in a professional to provide advice and structure.

How your MAGICIAN can hinder you: Making assumptions that your partner has your back because you're too busy inventing, creating and building new things.

How your JOKER can help you: Agree to book in some fun - whether it's lunch out or a romantic walk under the stars - for after the 'conversation about money' has concluded. Book it all in your calendar - in advance - at regular intervals.

How your JOKER can hinder you: Avoiding conversations about finances because they're boring (or because you fear it'll lead to an argument) can prove costly later.

How your ANGEL can help you: Offer to share the burden of looking after your joint finances with your partner - and mean it.

How your ANGEL can hinder you: Assuming that just like you, your partner will always have your best interests at heart. Indeed they may have - but that still doesn't mean that they necessarily know what they're doing.

How your ARCHITECT can help you: Cross check everything - regularly. Keep copies and record everything carefully - you'll be happier knowing that you can easily lay your hands on whatever information you may need, whenever you may need it.

How your ARCHITECT can hinder you: Believing that if the numbers are all in the right boxes on a spreadsheet, they must be right (after all, you double check everything carefully, so doesn't everyone else?).

How your PRISONER can help you: Recognise the trap of not being a party to what's going on with your joint finances and resolve to doing something about it. Often, just expressing the desire to learn (especially from someone who you believe knows more than you do) is enough to set the ball rolling.

How your PRISONER can hinder you: Feeling that you're simply not clever enough to be able to bring anything to the party when it comes to money keeps you trapped in the 'one down' position.

5 "IT'S JUST TOO LATE TO MAKE ANY DIFFERENCE TO MY FINANCES..."

There's often a point in our lives - irrespective of how many birthdays we've *actually* had - when we feel that we're running out of time. This particularly applies to the world of money - especially when you consider that many financial products like pensions rely on the magic of compound interest to make money grow over a long period of time.

But unless you're a time traveller, there's nothing you can do but accept that you are where you are *now*. Wringing your hands and wishing that you'd done things differently won't make any difference to your 'now'.

Indeed, learning from the past, accepting your current circumstances and deciding to make better decisions for the future is the wisest path you can take. You can also do some research - how have other people overcome the obstacles you're now facing?

In order to break free, recognise that making money the traditional way - through savings and investments - is not the only way! Your best resource is you - and the current invitation is for you to amplify your imagination and switch on your ingenuity.

How your PHARAOH can help you: Understand that *you* are your best resource - and see that the best time to start making a difference is **NOW**. The longest journey begins with the first step - and you're clever enough not to make this an overly long journey, right?

How your PHARAOH can hinder you: Believing that some outside agency - maybe an inheritance - will come to your rescue.

How your MAGICIAN can help you: Choose five areas in which you could make a small difference (however small that difference is) beginning today.

How your MAGICIAN can hinder you: Hoping that the next 'big idea' will resolve things - when actually, it's doing a number of smaller things which will make the biggest (and most sustainable) difference in the longer term.

How your JOKER can help you: Know that while it's important to have fun now, you'll also want to have fun in the future too. Commit to stacking up money in both your 'NOW' and 'FUTURE' bank accounts.

How your JOKER can hinder you: Adopting avoidance tactics - whether it's partying, keeping 'busy' or telling yourself that 'you never know how long you've got' - to prevent yourself from having to face the truth of the situation.

How your ANGEL can help you: Recognise that the greatest gift you can give others is *not being a burden on them* in the future. Start changing your behaviours now - and learn to say 'no' (most particularly with yourself. After all, your pay-off in spending your money looking after everyone else has been that it's made *you* feel needed. It's time for you to transcend that instant gratification now).

How your ANGEL can hinder you: Feeling needed is very important to you - and your unspoken hope is that because you've looked out for 'them', 'they' will look after *you* when the time comes. Know that they very well might NOT. What then?

How your ARCHITECT can help you: Research how other people have made the necessary changes in their financial circumstances to achieve the success you're looking for - and model their behaviours.

How your ARCHITECT can hinder you: Using the finer details to delude yourself that 'there'll be enough' when actually, you haven't challenged yourself to ask the 'bigger questions'.

How your PRISONER can help you: Step into your power and decide that you can make a difference. Once you make that decision, your subconscious mind will do all that it can to turn that decision into your new reality. Recognise too, that you'll be a role model for others - which will encourage them to step up as well.

How your PRISONER can hinder you: Allowing yourself to play the victim doesn't help anyone - least of all yourself.

6

"I'M SO DEEP IN DEBT - NOTHING I DO WILL MAKE ANY DIFFERENCE..."

It'll all too easy to get into debt - and often it's not just an addiction to the finer things in life that causes the problem. Just keeping a roof over your head and food on the table can sometimes only be accomplished with the use of a credit card. And however much you promise yourself that you'll pay it off soon, 'soon' never quite seems to arrive.

The result? Spiralling debt - often accompanied by what feels like crippling interest. Added to this is the shame you heap upon yourself for 'getting into this mess in the first place'.

Shame and guilt are both powerful emotions - and by making us uncomfortable, their purpose is to show us what doesn't make us feel good or happy, so that we'll avoid doing it again in the future. However, rather than just experiencing these emotions once and learning the lessons, what we usually do is repeatedly beat ourselves up and consequently lock ourselves into a negative and unhelpful cycle of powerlessness.

In order to break free, accept responsibility for the circumstances in which you currently find yourself (even if you don't see it as your 'fault', you've still played a role in how things unfolded). Accepting responsibility means that you reclaim your sovereignty - and therefore your power. Then, resolve to do things differently and start by making a plan for how you're going to clear your debt situation. (Hint: Allocate any spare resources to the debt with the highest interest first, after all, this is the one that's costing you the most money.)

How your PHARAOH can help you: Decide that you're the one in charge - and acknowledge that you've got the power to fix this. Embrace that power by taking *action*.

How your PHARAOH can hinder you: Ignoring the truth of the situation because of your chronic - if unspoken - sense of 'entitlement'. Alternatively, shame and worrying what other people might think can also keep you stuck in a world of damaging 'pretence'.

How your MAGICIAN can help you: Rather than going for the 'big deal', spot the smaller problems that other people are currently facing and work out how you can help them (and get paid for providing that help!). All the money you need already exists, it's just that currently, it's sitting in other people's bank accounts. Now all you have to do is work out how to provide enough value to make them *want* to give their money to you.

How your MAGICIAN can hinder you: Putting all your resources into your latest big project, in the hope that this time, you'll be able to pull the rabbit out of the hat. Desperation never pays off.

How your JOKER can help you: Ask for help. And while it's unlikely that anyone is going to wipe out your debts just because you ask, there *are* ways to deal with debt that makes it more manageable. Find out from other people who've been there before you (and who have come out of the situation successfully) to share their secrets with you.

How your JOKER can hinder you: Ignoring the problem won't make it go away. It'll make it worse. Facing up to reality is the most powerful - and most effective - choice you can make.

How your ANGEL can help you: Choose to put yourself - and your financial needs - *first* rather than at the back of the queue. Consider too, the advice you'd give someone you love who found themselves in the same position that you're in now. Follow that advice yourself.

How your ANGEL can hinder you: Know that being overly 'selfless' and overly generous when you can't afford it leaves you with the debts, while people you've helped remain debt-free.

How your ARCHITECT can help you: Use your keen logic to work out a master plan. Pay extra off the most expensive debts first - and when the first one is cleared, that'll leave you with some additional cash which you can use to fast track the clearing of your next most expensive debt. Repeat til you're debt-free.

How your ARCHITECT can hinder you: Tinkering about at the edges s-lo-w-l-y because you haven't investigated other ways of clearing your debts faster, can be a costly mistake.

How your PRISONER can help you: Without self-judgment or self recrimination, consider how you got into your debt situation in the first place. What needs to change in your approach to life? Who around you isn't actually helping, whatever they may say? (Hint: When we're stuck, we often attract other people who are in the same situation as we are - and we draw some comfort from knowing that we're not alone. But this false sense of security simply keeps everyone locked in the same negative and unhappy situation. Break free!)

How your PRISONER can hinder you: Wallowing in self pity - and constantly repeating your tales of woe to anyone who'll listen will simply keep you stuck.

7 "I LOVE WORKING FOR MYSELF BUT MY BUSINESS DRAINS ALL MY CASH AND ENERGY..."

While we all know that the logical point of being in business is to make money, all too often our sense of 'purpose' takes over. We can then find ourselves hosting an almost blinding messianic dedication to our work, little recognising the cost to both ourselves, our loved ones - and our bank balance.

And while it's good, especially in the early days, to re-invest the profits while you grow your business, there has to come a point when you're able to reap the rewards.

But for those whose joy *is* spotting new opportunities and creating new businesses, it's all too easy to keep using every spare bit of cash to finance new projects - burning not only your financial reserves but also your energy and vitality. (Physical burnout often accompanies, or at least swiftly follows, financial burnout. Be wise to the signs and take avoiding action before it's too late.)

In order to break free, dedicate a percentage of everything you earn (additional to what you set aside for your tax bills) to save - or preferably invest - in something that doesn't rely on *your* efforts. This is a pot that you'll build for your (*not* your business's) future.

You future self will thank you.

Additionally, investing (however little) in something other than your own business, will help you feel more prosperous and confident in your own ability to make money, which will in turn increase your levels of optimism (which will then rub off on your prospective clients and customers - who'll be more inclined to respond favourably to you. And so a virtuous cycle is set up.)

How your PHARAOH can help you: Focus first on building a sustainable and profitable business, knowing that the 'shiny things' can come later. This will lead to you feeling even more successful ultimately because you'll be able to buy those 'shiny things' from **profits** (rather than from your operating budget).

How your PHARAOH can hinder you: Spending money you don't have to make you appear successful eats into the cash your business needs to grow.

How your MAGICIAN can help you: Whatever your money-making endeavour, decide from the outset to set a proportion of what you earn to one side - just so you know that you have your 'own back' if things get tough. And at some point they will. The most successful people are those who are able to weather the storm when it comes - because when the tides turn again, you're still open for business, unlike all the others who fell by the wayside.

How your MAGICIAN can hinder you: While backing yourself is often a good move, having all your financial eggs in one basket will ultimately lead to trouble. However creative, optimistic and full of self-belief you are, understand that there will always be some things that are just outside of your control - and to weather any unforeseen storms, you need to be able to get your hands on 'rainy day' money.

How your JOKER can help you: Set yourself targets - and only reward yourself when you've achieved them.

How your JOKER can hinder you: Wasting money on things you don't need to compensate for the hard work and long hours you're putting in quickly drains your resources. Resist!

How your ANGEL can help you: Choose to make your business your priority - and give it the same care, attention and cash that you've previously been lavishing on your loved ones. Look after the 'cash-cow' **first** - and then it can look after you and your loved ones.

How your ANGEL can hinder you: Rather than re-investing your profits to grow your business, you instead use any extra cash to treat those around you - or to help them out of a tight spot. This ultimately will result in **you** being left in a tight spot.

How your ARCHITECT can help you: Pay yourself first - set up a regular payment to your savings account so that you know all your personal bills (and taxes) will be taken care of, leaving you free to focus on building the business. And as the business grows, then set up a savings (and/or investment) account which will be funded by your profits. Oh, and remember to put aside some of your profit for fun stuff too.

How your ARCHITECT can hinder you: Staying in your comfort zone and endlessly planning and measuring your activities means you get to avoid taking action. And it's action that brings in more revenue to your business.

How your PRISONER can help you: Decide where you can add value to what you do - so that you can confidently *increase your prices* and make your customers and clients even happier.

How your PRISONER can hinder you: Lacking in self belief, you're inclined to under charge - or worse, to offer discounts - which means that you're having to work unnecessarily hard just to stand still. When you offer a discount, it means you're 'selling on price' - and if your competitors do the same, it'll result in an expensive 'race to the bottom' in which everyone loses.

"PEOPLE TELL ME THAT EVEN THOUGH I'M SMART, I'M NOT REACHING MY FULL POTENTIAL…"

It can feel really heartbreaking when deep down, you sense that you're destined for 'bigger things' and yet on the face of it, you're seemingly stuck in a life of what feels like mediocrity.

An inner voice may be screaming that it wants to be set free - but the grind of every day seems to just keep you stuck.

While it's tempting to blame it on circumstances or the demands and needs of the people around you, know that when you do, you're giving your power away. While it's true that some people may rely on you, don't use that as an excuse not to live to your full potential. And while it's also true that other people (usually older, family members) may feel that they know what's best for you, again, don't use that as an excuse not to live up to your full potential.

Know too, that people often project their hopes, dreams and aspirations on to those around them - sometimes in a bid to be encouraging but more often to *make themselves feel better about what they haven't achieved themselves*. Make sure that it's your own path that you're seeking to follow, not one that someone else is mistakenly attempting to lay out for you.

Only you know what's right for you.

In order to break free, you're going to have to take some *risk*. You need to have to step out of your comfort zone - after all, what got you to 'here' isn't going to get you to 'there'. Maybe you'll also have to give up other people's good opinion of you in the short term - but know that when you've made it big, they'll be the first ones hanging on your sleeve, telling you that they knew all along that you 'could do it'!

Finally, rather than feel despondent, choose instead to take it as a compliment when other people tell you that you're not living up to your full potential - after all, they're effectively *agreeing with you* that you're capable of so much more, aren't they?

How your PHARAOH can help you: Know that success in life comes down to relationships. Work out how you can help other people achieve their goals, and they'll help you achieve yours. Practice your listening skills.

How your PHARAOH can hinder you: Believing you're smart doesn't mean that the world will automatically beat a path to your door.

How your MAGICIAN can help you: Choose one idea and focus on it exclusively. Use your creativity to make that idea as profitable and successful as you can (rather than wasting your creativity on shiny, new - but unrelated - ideas).

How your MAGICIAN can hinder you: Having too many ideas - however great they are - prevents you from completing any of them.

How your JOKER can help you: Decide how you want your working life to look and then consider who can best help you get there. Success comes through relationships. Build them.

How your JOKER can hinder you: Distracting yourself from the job in hand may make you feel better in the moment, but it prevents you from taking the actions that'll get you to where you know you truly deserve to be.

How your ANGEL can help you: Learn to look after yourself first. Your Angel wants you to look after *you*! Focus on what you need to get done and honour your promises. Make yourself your priority (for other people this might indeed be selfish, but for Angels, it's a *must*).

How your ANGEL can hinder you: Allowing other people's 'needs' takes your eye off the ball in your own court. Give up your need to be needed. It's disempowering - both to you and very often to the people you think you're helping.

How your ARCHITECT can help you: Schedule in time each day for meditation or for doing something creative just for the joy of it. Explore a variety of subjects that are outside your comfort zone - after all, the best ideas often come from a cross-fertilisation of different cultures or industries.

How your ARCHITECT can hinder you: Relying solely on logic means that you don't get to tap into your intuition or inner genius. Great leaps in progress often originate from the heart, rather than the head.

How your PRISONER can help you: Look for role models who have trodden the path before you. Learn from them - and apply the relevant lessons from their strategy to your life. Start now.

How your PRISONER can hinder you: Feeling that life is unfair - and that the world owes you a living (or should somehow 'discover' you) - simply keeps you stuck in the same dispiriting patterns of victimhood.

"ALL MY TIME, MONEY AND ENERGY GOES INTO LOOKING AFTER THE PEOPLE I CARE ABOUT..."

Sometimes life is just tough - and we just need to do what needs to be done to take care of those we love.

But when it becomes a perpetual pattern, it suggests that there's something else going on. Constantly putting your needs behind everyone else's **will** lead to burn out or illness (and very possibly both) - but long before you get there, you'll be experiencing anger, depression and resentment.

Doesn't sound like much fun, does it?

So ask yourself what hidden pay-off you're actually getting from all this over-generosity with your time, attention, energy and money. Does it secretly feel good to have people rely on you? Does it falsely bolster your confidence, knowing that they can't live without you (so they'll never leave you)? Or is it a lack of self-worth that's causing you to leave yourself out of the equation? Are you trying to make up for not feeling 'good enough'? Is a lack of self-confidence in your worth leading you to accept a lower reward than you deserve in your paid employment - or from your business clients?

In order to break free, the first step is to recognise what's going on and why. Recognise that you are at 'cause' rather than 'effect' - and this will enable you to take back your own power. Then decide what you need - and want - and choose to put yourself first. After all, the only person who gets to live your life is...**you**!

How your PHARAOH can help you: Learn the art of delegation - and you'll quickly prosper.

How your PHARAOH can hinder you: Acting as the benefactor and figurehead for your tribe requires deep pockets. It can also disempower those around you. Ask yourself whether the 'feeling good about yourself' pay-off is actually worth the financial, emotional and energetic **cost to you**.

How your MAGICIAN can help you: Invite those around you to work out how they can solve their own problems. Sure, they can use you as a sounding board for their ideas - but make sure to schedule a 'stop-time' for these discussions (to avoid them becoming endless).

How your MAGICIAN can hinder you: Being able to see future possible outcomes - for both yourself and others - can be a double edged sword. While spotting opportunities is great for business, spotting what could go wrong for everyone around you (and leaping into action to prevent it from happening) reduces *their* ability to take care of themselves. And as you've already found out, it also drains you and your wallet.

How your JOKER can help you: Plan fun time into your calendar - along with work time. That way, you'll avoid distraction and you'll soon be on course to achieve your goals and objectives.

How your JOKER can hinder you: Having fun or spending your own time and money to cheer up the people around you distracts you from doing what's important for *you*. Sure, do it on occasion, but make sure that you're not actually being 'generous' in a bid to avoid doing the work that'll make that all-important difference to your own life and business!

How your ANGEL can help you: Know that the kindest thing you can do for others is to be self-sufficient, especially financially. Just as importantly, take into account your own future 'needs'. You won't want to be a burden on others in the future, so make sure you won't be by ensuring that you're setting enough aside for yourself now.

How your ANGEL can hinder you: Enjoying an inflated sense of 'importance' because everyone seemingly needs you is the fastest way to drain your energy - and your bank account.

How your ARCHITECT can help you: Ask for help. Other people love being invited to 'step up' and will enjoy the fact that you trust them with the responsibility. Knowing that you're not alone with it all will free you to do what you do best: plan and implement for success.

How your ARCHITECT can hinder you: Focusing constantly on all your responsibilities and commitments can weigh you down - leaving you feeling overwhelmed and overburdened. This saps your energy, which makes it harder to go out there and do your thing. In time, your bank account gets sapped too, and before you know it, you're living in a vicious, expensive and unhappy cycle.

How your PRISONER can help you: Set a budget - in terms of both your time *and* your money - which will show you how much you actually have available for others (and how much you need to keep for yourself). This way, not only will you recognise your boundaries, but it'll be easier to reinforce them too.

How your PRISONER can hinder you: Feeling as though it's only other people who benefit from your hard work and ability to earn money is a downward spiral - and it will only stop when you realise that it's *you* who is allowing it to happen.

IMAGINE IF MONEY COULD SPEAK - WHAT WOULD IT SAY YOU?

As you know by now, it's my belief that Money is one of the greatest teaching tools on this planet - after all, it's a mirror on which we project our hopes and fears, along with a myriad of other emotions.

I've often thought that it would be really cool if we could have a conversation with Money - what would it have to say to us, and about our relationship with it?

What would Money want to say to *you*?

Intriguingly, not long after I recognised that Money was such a powerful teacher, I found myself becoming its intermediary in client sessions. Speaking on behalf of Money in this way - like it's Ambassador if you will, feels like a privilege - and I'm always completely stunned by how quickly these conversations create profound and lasting shifts for everyone involved.

If you'd like to get a free "Message from Money" every weekday, then you can do so here: https://oliviastefanino.com/messages-from-money

Overleaf, you'll find what Money has to say to each of the six 'Money Types':

Money's Message for the Pharaoh:

"Remember that your role in the world is as a LEADER - and the most profitable place to start your journey is with **you**. To lead yourself, you need to know yourself - and must make the transition from your ego to your heart. Use logic and knowledge - but combine them with intuition and compassion. Rule with wisdom. Claim your sovereignty, know what you want to achieve - but be wary of measuring your own self worth by how much money you've got in the bank. Remember that unlike the Ancient Egyptian Pharaohs, you can't take it with you - so use money wisely. You have been gifted the good fortune of being able to build wealth easily - and while it's there to be enjoyed by you, it's not for your sole use. Share it, help others with it, show others how to follow in your footsteps."

Money's Message for The Magician

"Remember that your role in the world is as a CREATOR. Hold a vision of the life you'd like to create - and who or what you want your creations to **serve.** Your journey to success begins with you. As you grow and learn more about yourself, you will make the transition from your ego to your heart. Use vision, intuition and compassion - but combine them with logic and knowledge to create wisdom. Before embarking on any other projects, first create your own secure financial platform or 'cash cow' so that you can seed fund your ideas, free from personal financial worry. You have been gifted the good fortune of being both a creator and a visionary - and while these gifts are to be enjoyed by you, they're not for your sole use. Share them, help others with them, show others how to follow in your footsteps."

Money's Message for The Joker

"Remember that your role in the world is to CELEBRATE LIFE. Hold a vision of building a life that is worth celebrating - and make an action plan for its manifestation. The journey to success begins with you. As you grow and learn more about yourself, you will make the transition from your ego to your heart. Use vision, intuition and gratitude - but combine them with logic and knowledge to create wisdom. Know that relationships and collaboration are the key to your success - and as a currency, are worth more to you than the money you have in the bank. Invest in your relationships with generosity.

Know that you will look back and see how easy it was for you to earn money in the moment. Be generous with your 'future you' by saving enough money now. You have been gifted the good fortune of being easily able to generate money through relationships - but while this gift is to be enjoyed by you, it is not for your sole use. Share it, help others with it, show others how to follow in your footsteps."

Money's Message for The Angel

"Remember that your role in the world is as a PEACEMAKER. Guiding, helping and holding the space for others comes naturally to you - but you will profit the most from learning to take as much care of yourself. Drop the fear that looking after yourself is selfish. When you are self sufficient, you do not burden others. The more you have, the more you can share. Strengthen your personal boundaries. Take care of your needs now, save for the future - and only then share what's left with others. Money is a tool - and when you operate from the heart rather than your ego, you are able to achieve what many would consider 'impossible'. Use intuition, empathy and compassion - but combine them with logic and knowledge to create wisdom. You have been gifted the good fortune of foresight and humanity - but while these gifts are to be enjoyed by you, they are not for your sole use. Share them with others, and help yourself too. Show others how to follow in your footsteps."

Money's Message for The Architect

"Remember that your role in the world is as a PLANNER. Inspire yourself with a vision of how you would like life to be, and then make a detailed plan for action. The journey to success begins with you. As you grow and learn about yourself, you will make the transition from your ego to your heart. Use logic and knowledge - but combine them with intuition and generosity of spirit to create wisdom. Recognise that you can only get so far doing things on your own. The biggest projects are achieved in collaboration with others. Articulate the vision, create a blueprint and then build the foundations. Learn to see the big picture and the finer details simultaneously. Avoid the temptation of adventurous schemes - you profit from sticking to the plan. Practice the art of knowing where you can make savings and when it's prudent to invest. Putting a considered amount of money aside regularly for your future self brings confidence and security - leaving you mentally free to focus on your current work. You have been gifted the good fortune of being able to strategise and build wealth steadily - and while these gifts are to be enjoyed by you, they're not for your sole use. Share them, help others with them, show others how to follow in your footsteps."

Money's Message for The Prisoner

"Remember that your role in the world is as a LIBERATOR. You see what isn't working and that brings you *choice*. Do you join the crowd, complaining and wringing your hands in self-pity? NO - challenge yourself to create a better way! Know that as you create freedom for yourself from the past, you in turn set hope alight in others. The journey to success begins with you. As you grow and learn about yourself, you will make the transition from your ego to your heart. Use logic and knowledge - but combine them with intuition and generosity of spirit to create wisdom. Money doesn't buy you happiness but it can get you freedom. Recognise that Money is not your enemy - and never has been. Know that Money likes hanging around with people who appreciate it rather than resent it. Money exists to help you build, to create and to leave a legacy. Choose to leave the world a better place than you found it. Establish your boundaries, energise your mindset and be inspired by the stories of others who have overcome hardship and turned their lives around. Take charge, become the director of your own personal 'life movie' and know that in turn, you'll be the inspiration for others. You have been gifted the good fortune of being able to see what the world needs and to understand the power of freedom. While these gifts are to be enjoyed by you, they're not for your sole use. Share them, help others with them, show others how to follow in your footsteps."

ABOUT THE AUTHOR

Olivia Stefanino has been on the fringes of the world of business and finance for more than two decades – initially as a journalist and subsequently as a speaker, executive coach and leadership specialist.

Working with some of the finance profession's biggest institutions – from a couple of high street banks through to MBNA and what were then Skandia and Norwich Union – she's come to see why some people succeed, while others fall by the wayside.

Her credo is that 'successful companies employ successful individuals' - and her transformational work with both large organisations and smaller companies results in increased profits and improved employee engagement and wellbeing.

In her first book, "*Be Your Own Guru – personal and business enlightenment in just 3 days!*", Olivia shares the story of a pilot project with a high street bank in which her innovative approach helped the organisation's sales team to improve their profits by a massive 330% (and absenteeism went down).   Smaller companies working with Olivia also see dramatic results too – in just one example, a restaurant owner was amazed to find profits had quadrupled in less than six months.

Interviewed on numerous radio programmes, Olivia has also been featured in "The Guardian", the "Financial Times" and "Red" Magazine, as well as in a variety of other publications.

Testimonials for Olivia...

"Our organisation invested in over two years of Olivia's input and the results were phenomenal. As well as a 20% growth in revenue and a 6% market share growth in a diminishing industry, we also saw a 30% improvement in sales productivity."

Steve Dunstan, former general manager, Genus/ABS PLC

"As well as acting as a roving mentor and Dragon for us recently, Olivia is a guest lecturer for my students each year - and we all really love her 'Money Types' system!"

Jonathan Styles, Lecturer, Mentor & Master of Enterprise at The Business School, University of Manchester

"Olivia was a breath of fresh air, someone who wanted to get to the heart of the company and understand its culture and how we could improve things. No lectures or text book management training but, straight forward, hard hitting advice to help us in 'Creating a Juicier Future'. With Olivia's help, we have achieved objectives hitherto unattainable."

Sheila Davie, Human Resources Manager, Calypso Soft Drinks

"Olivia has heart and soul which is filled with inspiration, emotional intelligence and compassion – all bound with a wonderful sense of humour, which she uses to guide you through virtually anything. I've recommended her as a speaker to a number of my corporate clients - and they've all reported back that the events were a great success. On a personal note, Olivia has given me tools to help me stop being being a 'people pleaser', and I now feel a lot more in control of my own destiny and inflows of money."

Lynn Pates, Charities Investment Consultant, LKP Consultants

"As an experienced coach who sometimes needs coaching, I have been bowled over by Olivia's approach. She has the knack of asking excellent questions, of kindly and humorously keeping me on track while also encouraging me to think big. At the same time she is full of ideas which are specific to my own needs, and she's not afraid to give them away."

Pippa Addamson, Advanced Lightning Process Practitioner and Change Coach

"Olivia has skills in so many areas, it's hard to know where to begin. Her star asset, however, is the gift of inspiring...of making people feel they can achieve the desired results. Olivia combines wisdom and compassion with a very focused and practical approach - aimed at securing clients' goals. Corporate clients, particularly, will benefit from the sheer breadth and spectrum of her knowledge and experience. Also, she's got a wonderful warm sense of humour!"

Merryn Myatt, Myatt-Perris Media

"Olivia is intuitive, inspirational and basically a genius. She has taught me about my relationship with money, and has blown my mind with how powerful this can be when you understand and use it appropriately."

Sarah Rugg, Founder of Vi-Va

"Tapping into the wisdom of the 'Money Types', with Olivia's guidance, has been beyond incredible. Understanding my emotional relationship with Money has enabled me to take my online business to the next level & has given me the freedom to work from wherever I choose!"

Kelly Cox, Creator & Digital Coach at The Green Thread

"Olivia is a magical genius. Pay close attention to everything she has to say."

Lynda Mangoro – Creative Genie

Lightning Source UK Ltd.
Milton Keynes UK
UKHW020713170919
349927UK00007B/307/P